THE NEW BBC BOOK OF
BOWLS

THE NEW BBC BOOK OF
BOWLS

Keith Phillips

BBC BOOKS

Published by BBC Books,
A division of BBC Enterprises Ltd
Woodlands, 80 Wood Lane, London W12 0TT

First published 1990

© The Contributors and BBC Enterprises Ltd 1990

ISBN 0 563 20896 1

Typeset in 10/11½pt Goudy
by Ace Filmsetting Ltd, Frome

Printed and bound in Great Britain by Richard Clay Ltd, Bungay

Cover printed by Richard Clay Ltd, Norwich

PICTURE ACKNOWLEDGEMENTS

Front cover of David Corkill © Eric Whitehead

Page 65 BBC; 92 and 93 Bowlers' World; 13, 24, 25, 37, 53, 57, 59, 61, 67, 71, 75, 79, 87, 98, 100 and 105 Duncan Cubitt/Bowls International; 17 Jimmy Davidson; 83, 89, 101, 103 Greenall Whitley Waterloo Bowling/Jack Leigh; 8, 9 and 10 The Hulton-Deutsch Collection; 121 Keith Phillips; 35 David Rhys Jones; 115 and 123 Patrick Sullivan; 40 and 51 Bob Thomas Sports Photography; 16, 38, 41, 43, 47, 48 and 62 Eric Whitehead.

CONTENTS

INTRODUCTION

Some years have passed since the first BBC *Book of Bowls* was published and, despite one or two teething problems, I think it successfully filled its brief. This book is a sequel to the first edition, not only updating what has been happening in the bowling world since 1986, but also bringing some fresh points of interest to the reader's attention. There are new chapters by the World Championship sponsors and by our own television presenter David Icke, who is now an active member of the Green Party – excuse the non-intended pun.

My colleagues Jimmy Davidson and David Rhys Jones have contributed once again, adding some new ideas over the following chapters. There is also a new chapter on the Ladies' game in both level and crown green bowling.

From the point of television exposure, crown green has suffered rather badly and we are now left with just one tournament on the BBC – the Waterloo Handicap. Flat green bowling has fared little better, with only the UK Singles Indoor Championship and the combined World Singles and Pairs Indoor Championships televised on the BBC.

Nevertheless, the game of bowls is steadily gaining in popularity and, while the outdoor level green game has maintained a constant membership, the indoor game is flourishing, recruiting a large number of crown green members during their close season.

Once again, my aim in the *New BBC Book of Bowls* is to entertain, educate and inform, and I hope that you will enjoy reading it.

I would like to express my appreciation for the help given to me by the contributors and to acknowledge the following people, without whose assistance this book would probably not have 'made the air'.

David Harrison – Tournament Director and Contracts Executive for the WIBC

Jimmy Barclay – Assistant Secretary of the WIBC and Convenor of Umpires for the WIBC and BIIBC

Frank Kitchen – Bowls Organiser for the WIBC

Mary Ashcroft – Ladies' referee and organiser of the Ladies' Waterloo

Jack Leigh – Manager, Waterloo Bowls

Terry Magee – Editor, Bowlers' World

Margaret Johnston – Irish International bowler

Norma Shaw – English International bowler

Terry Nichols – Vice Chairman and Cheshire representative on the BCGRS

I would also like to thank all the players whose profiles appear in this book and my wife Susan who, once again, worked into the night to put the manuscript on to the word processor.

KEITH PHILLIPS
November 1989

A SHORT HISTORY OF THE GAME

Keith Phillips

On the walls of Ancient Egyptian temples can be found images of people playing what looks remarkably like a form of bowls, using skittles and rounded stones. Although these are, as far as we know, the earliest records of this type of game, Man's instinctive urge to throw rounded objects at predesignated targets – witness a child on the beach, who will almost immediately want to pitch pebbles into the water – makes it likely that similar games have been in existence since the very beginning of our appearance on earth.

Furthering the Egyptian theory, it is thought that the game was passed via traders, as well as occupying armies, to other early civilisations, eventually reaching Europe. A more gruesome version of early bowls was played by the Mongols who swept across Europe at the fall of the Roman empire. They used the heads of their defeated enemies as 'woods'. Drawings depicting a very similar game, also using human heads, can be found in Mexico, dating back to the Aztecs.

The origin of bowls as we know it today, can be traced to the

Sir Francis Drake at Plymouth Hoe

8

Medieval game of Jacti Lapidum, which involved throwing stones at a target. It is thought that the bowling term 'jack' derives directly from Jacti.

In England bowling seems to have been enjoyed immensely by the monarchy. One of the earliest recorded references to the game was uttered by King John. 'Talk not of bowls,' he said. 'What is life but a game of bowls in which the King is all too frequently knocked down.' Henry VIII also indulged in the pastime, although he forbade his subjects to play. It is thought that he was concerned that it would interfere with their archery practice. At that time, skilled archers were, of course, essential on the battlefield.

The most famous historical bowling incident on record occurred in the summer of 1588. Britain had been at war with Spain for many years, and knew that the arrival of Philip's mighty fleet was imminent. Sir Francis Drake, second-in-command of the English fleet, was enjoying a game of bowls when news of the sighting of the Spanish Armada off the Isles of Scilly reached him. As his playing companions brought the game to a halt, probably feeling a sense of urgency at the impending invasion, he is reputed to have said, 'They must wait their turn, good souls,' and as legend has it, he went on to lose the game!

William Shakespeare, himself a bowls player, made several references to it in his work. For instance, in *Richard II*, as the Queen is walking in the Duke of York's garden, she remarks to

King Charles I (seated) attending a game of bowls

her lady companions, 'What sport shall we devise here in this garden to drive away the heavy thought of care?' 'Madam, shall we play bowls?' suggests one of the ladies.

Apart from the games enjoyed by the aristocracy, bowls has, until recent years, had a very bad reputation indeed. Usually played at ale houses, it was associated with drunkenness and gambling. Participants were considered to be of the 'lower orders', and to be lazy and aggressive. The latter was probably true, because in the late 1800s a Scottish lawyer named W.W. Mitchell introduced a law forbidding 'kicking, hacking and tripping' by the players.

There is a charming story of how the now essential 'bias' of the bowls was first introduced. It dates back to the time when the bowls were made out of solid wood. Charles Brandon, Duke of Suffolk, was playing a game at Goole, in Yorkshire. One of the Duke's bowls was hit by that of an opponent, and it fell in two halves. Rather than retire from the game, he ran outside the house – which was not his own – and sawed the spherical knob off the bottom of the banister in the grand hall! Returning to the game, the Duke discovered that the flattened part of the knob, where it had been attached to the banister, made it run in an arch, thus enabling him to 'see' the jack!

A rural game of bowls (1870)

ASSOCIATION BOWLS

Despite strong pockets of resistance, bowls became organised, standardised and respectable as 'lawn bowling'. In this sanitised form, it was exported to Australia and other, mainly Commonwealth, countries.

Back home, one of the main areas to hold out against the pressures to regiment bowls was the North West of England. In that area the lads continued to play on improvised surfaces, and resisted all pressures to make greens standard and level. Crown green bowlers have always jealously guarded their independence from mainstream, level green bowls. Indeed they proudly regard themselves as mainstream! In the North East of England and in East Anglia, at the turn of the century, they also spurned the new up-market image of bowls and rejected the association game.

The game has developed widely this century. Indoor bowls has become popular; women's bowls has strengthened in numbers, and each of the four home countries has its own national administration. One particularly strong branch of indoor bowls, and a product of this century, is short mat bowls. It thrives in Ireland and South Wales and is gaining popularity in many parts of England.

For the newcomer, here is a brief guide to the 'mainstream' of bowls today:

IBB/WIBC (association) bowls is the truly international game: the one played outdoors on grass or indoors on carpets both on *flat* surfaces – and is featured on television in such major events as *Jack High*, the World Indoor Singles and Pairs, and the UK Championship. It is the game that W.W. Mitchell wrote the rules for, the game that Dr W.G. Grace liked so much that he founded the English Bowling Association in 1903, and the game which the general public has come to identify with.

Outdoor bowls (IBB Association Bowls)
The World Championships are held at four-year intervals (Aberdeen 1984, Auckland 1988, Worthing 1992) in between the Commonwealth Games contests (Brisbane 1982, Edinburgh 1986 and Auckland 1990). England and Australia are the strongest countries in terms of numbers of players, although

both Scotland and New Zealand would hotly dispute claims of world domination in terms of achievement. South Africa, too, given the chance, would be very much in the running as a top bowls country, while Canada, USA, Hong Kong, Israel, Ireland and Wales can also muster strong teams.

The IBB laws of the game specify a square green, with sides measuring between 40 and 44 yards. Each rink is between 18 and 19 feet wide, and the green is surrounded by a ditch between two and eight inches deep.

Competitions are arranged for single-handed play, pairs, triples or fours, or for teams. The home international series, for example, requires national teams to put five teams of four players on the green. A match between England and Scotland, with 40 keyed-up players crowding the green, is always an intense, competitive and noisy affair.

Most bowls, however, is played at club level. Generally the format is team-play, each four in the team comprising lead, second, third and skip. Each player delivers two woods, so there are 16 bowls in the head when each end is complete. In triples even more woods build up – 18 in all or three per player – while in pairs and singles each player as a rule uses four bowls.

Club bowls in England is flourishing. At the last count, in 1986, there were 2,683 clubs with 121,630 players, associated to the English Bowling Association.

Unlike crown and federation, few association clubs are nowadays attached to pubs and hostelries. However, whether it is a private or a parks club, the social side of bowls is still of vital importance. Most clubs have a clubhouse with bar, where the 22nd end is the equivalent of golf's 19th hole – the place for post-mortems over a pint.

The EBA championships are held every year at Beach House Park in Worthing. Not surprisingly, David Bryant is England's most prolific championship winner, having bagged an extraordinary 16 titles since 1957.

Thirty-five counties are affiliated to the EBA, ranging in size from lowly Lancashire, with eight clubs, to Surrey with 213. The only English counties without flat green EBA bowls are Cheshire, Shropshire and Staffordshire, which are firmly entrenched in the crown green code.

Indoor bowls (WIBC – Association Bowls)

Indoor bowls began over a century ago as a makeshift winter substitute for the summer lawn game. In 1888 in Drumdryan Drill Hall, Scotsman William Macrae girded his bowls with rubber bands and experimented on a sawdust-covered concrete floor. Years later Edinburgh folk bowled by gaslight in the cellars of the Synod Hall. The bearded W.G. Grace was influential in founding an indoor club at Crystal Palace in 1906.

Today indoor bowls in booming. The game is played in great stadiums on green carpets, 40 yards square and as smooth as the best snooker tables. There are now over 200 indoor clubs in England, 32 in Scotland, ten in Wales and four in Ireland.

Embassy have been connected with the World Indoor Singles since 1979. CIS have sponsored the UK Singles since 1983, and were generous bowls benefactors before that. Midland Bank joined in in 1986, sponsoring the first World Indoor Pairs Championship at Bournemouth.

Rules are virtually the same as outdoors. It *is*, some say, the same game. Usually a good player on grass is also a good player on carpet. But like all rules there are exceptions, and while bowlers like Willy Wood, Chris Ward, Jimmy Hobday and David Cutler seem to prefer the great outdoors, others like Terry Sullivan, Jim Baker, David Corkill, Roy Cutts, and, to some extent, Tony Allcock, perform more happily with a roof over their heads.

The EBA championships at Beach House Park, Worthing

13

Outdoor bowls (EBF – Federation Bowls)

The English Bowling Federation was founded in 1926, but its origins go back much further. Now played in 13 English counties from Northumberland to Essex, federation bowls may be less sophisticated than its EBA counterpart, but it is just as vigorous in its own way.

Federation bowlers normally bowl with two woods, in team games as well as singles. They do not play fours, and tend to call their basic two-wood triples game 'rinks'. They do not insist that their surfaces conform to such strict standards as their EBA rivals, and they are more tolerant to the concept of mixed bowling – indeed they encourage it.

An emphasis on drawing to the jack is encouraged by the ruling 'no bowl shall count which lays more than six feet from the jack'. There are no 'touchers'. Federation bowlers are understandably proud of their drawing ability.

Championship finals are held at Skegness every August. Since federation bowls is confined to England, there are no British or international events, so top federation bowlers often join EBA clubs to further their ambitions. Chris and David Ward, Roy Cutts and John Ottaway are among today's top stars who were brought up on the EBF game.

OUTDOOR BOWLS (CROWN GREEN)

The roving jack principle of crown green bowls firmly puts crown green as, probably, the most genuine and natural form of bowls. Crown green tournaments were popular on television long before the current growth of the top flat events had been envisaged and spectator participation has always been a feature of crown.

Crown green bowlers share many skills with their flat green counterparts, but the strategy of the two codes is quite different. Indeed, crown green bowls is such a unique, independent game that it earns a full chapter in its own right (see page 76).

INDOOR BOWLS (SHORT MAT)

Rain stopped play. This familiar sporting scourge sent two teams of Belfast bowlers seeking shelter in a church hall. The hall was carpeted. 'Why not ...?' thought the enterprising Irish – and the short mat game was born in 1926! There are now 900 clubs in Ireland, catholic *and* protestant, north *and* south of the border, with over 40,000 estimated members.

A similar thing happened in Wales. Bowls fanatics in the Rhondda moved indoors in the winter so that they could bowl all year round. They, too, rolled out mats in church halls and working men's clubs, and formed the WIBA in 1934.

At first, the mats were all shapes and sizes, but gradually some order was imposed to regulate a booming pastime. The IIBA was formed in 1961, and the short mat people *still* use the initials, jealously denying them to the 'proper', full-size green, national body.

While the Welsh went all respectable (a full-size stadium in Cardiff) or played an ad hoc hybrid game (there are only about 20 *genuine* short mat clubs in Wales), the Irish game grew and grew – and eventually crossed the Irish Sea. There are around 15 short mat clubs in the Stranraer area in Scotland, and the English Short Mat Bowling Association, formed in Stockport in 1984, now has almost 300 affiliated clubs.

Mats are between 40 and 50 feet long and only six feet wide. Although full-sized bowls are used, there are cross-boards to minimise 'firing' and, of course, no ditches. While some people might dismiss it as a toy game, there is certainly great interest and lively competition.

INDOOR BOWLS (PORTABLE RINK)

In the early 1980s, when television became interested in indoor bowls, it was decided that the existing small indoor clubs were not really suitable venues. Producers had already learned from snooker, which was first widely televised in the late 1970s, that people would want to come and watch this new spectacle in increasingly large numbers. The small indoor clubs could only hold between 200 and 300 people, and thousands now wanted to see this new bowling phenomenon. To fulfil the new requirements, Mike Watterson and David Harrison, a promoter who is now the WIBC Tournament and Media Director, invented the concept of the portable indoor rink.

The rink was originally designed by a Bristolian called Mike Williams and was first used in the CIS UK Indoor Champion-

Installing a portable indoor rink at Bournemouth

ship in 1983 at the Preston Guild Hall. There were many teething troubles with the rink, and the design had to be modified two or three times before it was just about perfected in 1986. One of the initial problems was it took three days to build. Now it takes less than a day, and in the 1989 CIS UK Indoor Championship, David Bryant said he 'hadn't played on a truer and more perfect rink anywhere.' It is possible that one of the reasons for his praise was the new lighting system provided by the WIBC and the Guild Hall at Preston.

TARGET BOWLS

The newest innovation in the short mat game is Target Bowls. Initially, as a game for drawing practice, it attracted great interest when the BBC children's sports programme *Move It* staged a championship for rookie 11-year-olds in 1988. The 16 players had two hours' coaching before taking part in the televised tournament. The Championship was staged again in 1989 and in 1990 it is being extended to a National Tournament.

In Target Bowls, the jack is replaced by a red and yellow target four-feet in diameter, with scoring circles arranged from one point for an outer to 10 points for a bull. The delivery mat is placed 20 yards from the target and moved back as the players improve their scoring.

16

HOW TO PLAY

Jimmy Davidson

PLAYING TRENDS IN THE GAME

It is now almost a full decade since bowls went 'open'; a player could, if he wished, retain his amateur status by refusing prize money in excess of his expenses – but there are not many Corinthian Casuals about these days! Nowadays, top players would feel complimented to be told they had adopted an increasingly professional approach to the game and the attendant pressures.

Players have responded magnificently to the challenges of television and new scoring systems. One feature that surprises new competitors in a televised event on the portable rink, is that the packed house means that the audience is claustrophobically close to the bowler. For a crown green bowler, this is most evident at the Superbowl. Even competing at the Waterloo finals before 4,000 spectators would not be adequate preparation for a packed Granada Stage One. Walking 40 yards down a narrow channel of spectators, in a cacophony of noise so unnervingly

close to you, is not the same as competing in a game of bowls on the 50 yard square stage at Blackpool.

One of the best aids to assist players' concentration has been the introduction of the sets scoring system. It was first introduced to television audiences in 1982 in the Triple Crown Classic, transmitted by what was then Southern Television. Sets of nine shots were tried in that event, but

Jimmy Davidson

17

for succeeding events, sets of seven shots have become the accepted norm. The most frequent comment heard from players on their introduction to sets play is 'You can't afford to play any loose bowls' – and they're right.

Close-up television pictures give viewers plenty of opportunity to see the grimaces of concentration on the best-known bowling faces. It is almost as if the players are in pain, so intense are the thought-processes as they visualise the shot they are about to play.

My final example of developing playing trends and tactics stems directly from players' reactions to the new pressures of performing in front of television cameras. Some are astute enough to turn this pressure to their own advantage. Watch carefully, and you will sometimes spot a player 'turning the screw' in this way. When one of the players is in trouble with, for instance, a game-losing position against him, he does not want to hang around too long before attempting the shot which will, hopefully, save the game. In these circumstances, it is a legitimate tactic for the other player to let his opponent 'stew' a little, while he takes more time than usual to play his own final bowl.

A player facing this tactic should stay cool and take a few deep breaths while waiting. It is surprising how calming that extra intake of oxygen can be. I would be on your side – I like to see the biter bitten.

IT'S EASY TO LEARN

Bowls is a simple game, based on a fairly natural physical movement. It's easy to learn, and there are plenty of qualified instructors willing to teach absolute beginners. It invariably pleases and surprises novices that within a couple of hours of beginning their instruction, they can take part in a competitive game of bowls.

It has always been the case that any man, woman, boy or girl calling in at their local bowls club would find a member who would help them to learn to play. These days, in England alone, there are nearly 3,000 Certificated Instructors. They teach in accordance with the syllabus and guidelines of the English Bowls Coaching Scheme. The instruction they give is practical, on the green, and without any prior verbal discourse.

The object of the game is to get your bowl(s) nearer to the

jack than your opponent. The jack is the spherical white 'target' object, less than 1lb in weight and about two and a half inches in diameter. The jack is delivered first up to a maximum distance of 40 yards and a minimum of 25 yards. The first jack is delivered by the player who wins the toss; thereafter the winner of each game or 'end' bowls the jack first.

In the flat game, there are four different types of match: 1) Singles 2) Pairs 3) Triples 4) Fours. The scoring in each end of each match is the same; the nearest bowl(s) to the jack takes the point.

Singles Each player has four bowls and can, therefore, score up to four shots an end. Normally, the first to score 21 shots wins. Currently, in indoor televised tournaments, the players have to win a given number of 'sets'. A set is won by the first player to reach seven points.

Pairs There are two players per team. Each player has four bowls and 21 ends are played, with an extra end available in the event of a tie in the total number of shots scored. In some televised indoor tournaments, there are two-bowl pairs, which means that each player has two bowls and, in this format, the winners have to beat their opponents in a given number of sets, each set consisting of seven ends.

Triples Three players per team. Each player has three bowls and 18 ends are played, with an extra end in the event of a tie in the total number of shots scored.

Fours Four players per team. Each player has two bowls and 21 ends are played with an extra end available in the event of a tie in the total number of points scored.

In the crown green game each player always has two bowls and the scoring system is the same, ie the nearest bowl(s) to the jack wins. There are usually three different maximum points targets per match. Most games are played 21 up or 31 up, with some pairs competitions even going to 41 up, although this is not as common as competing for the lower scores.

EQUIPMENT AND BOWL SELECTION

The learner, who should dress in casual clothes, will be equipped with a pair of flat-soled shoes, or overshoes, and will be lent a set of four bowls to use.

There are eight different sizes of bowl, varying in diameter from 4⅝ inches to 5⅛ inches, and ranging in weight to a maximum of 3lb 8oz each. Each bowl of the set of four is identical, and all 'turn' the same amount on the same green. That is to say, the 'bias' of the four bowls has been matched precisely in manufacture.

The bias of different sets can vary. The rule is that every bowl must 'bend' more than a master bowl kept in each country. Instructors advise each beginner not to buy a set of bowls until they learn how to play, and have also found which make, weight and size suits them best.

A set of bowls will last a bowling lifetime. Costs vary, but the average price is in the order of about £100 for the set. This amount represents the major part of the total cost of preparing to play the game, socially or competitively.

DELIVERY ACTION

It is a fundamental principle of the English Bowls Coaching Scheme that every bowler's delivery action is as unique as their fingerprints. Although several actions can be categorised by a general description (eg Crouch, Athletic etc) each action is different in some detailed respect, from every other action. A further principle of the Scheme is that, to be acceptable, the adopted action of any beginner needs to satisfy three criteria:

a That it is comfortable, that is to say, it does not produce unnecessary strain and can be precisely repeated for long periods of play.

b That it is effective and will not be measured by theoretical imperatives related to its constituent parts.

c That it conforms with the laws of the game, ie that the whole of one foot is on, or directly above, the confines (24in × 14in) of the bowls mat at the precise moment at which the bowl leaves the hand.

Until recently, the method of instruction used to establish the delivery action which best suited each beginner, was to get the learner to copy demonstrations of several different types of action. The instructor and pupil then chose the action which seemed to be producing the best results.

This method of starting the instruction process was changed fairly recently in England. Now the beginner is invited to stand on the bowls mat and is given a jack. He or she is then asked to roll the jack to the instructor, who is positioned some seven to ten yards away.

The beginner's natural movement in rolling what is, to every one of them, a fairly familiar object to handle – a ball about the same size as a tennis ball – is what the instructor uses in helping the learner to groove in a bowls delivery action.

Repeated rolling of the jack over increased distances, is used by the instructor to build on that which is inherent and good, and to eliminate that which, if uncorrected, might produce error. Good stance, timing and rhythm may already be present, or can be produced by encouraging correction, in this repeated movement.

The instructor then varies the places where the beginner stands in relation to the mat, so that the learner has to vary his stance on the mat, changing the position of his feet to accommodate the new angles of delivery from the mat. Once an acceptable delivery action has been established using the jack, the beginner is then ready to repeat the action using a bowl. This is the point at which the instructor explains:

a Bias

b Forehand and Backhand

c Line and Length

Bias
It is the shape of a bowl which makes it turn. (Many spectators, even some bowlers, erroneously believe that one side of the bowl is more heavily weighted than the other.) As the bowl slows down, the surface on which the bowl runs turns towards the side on which the disc is the smaller.

21

The diagram on page 23 shows the forehand path of a bowl to a short jack, and a full-length jack. It can be seen that the first part of the route travelled to both lengths is the same. It is only at the point when the bowl loses impetus and begins to travel much more slowly that it begins to turn. This point is known as the 'shoulder' for that length of jack. It is usually about two-thirds of the distance towards the point at which the bowl will come to rest.

It will also be seen that the direction in which the bowl must be aimed is the same for the two different lengths of jack. This is known as the line on that hand or that rink (number two in this case) of that green.

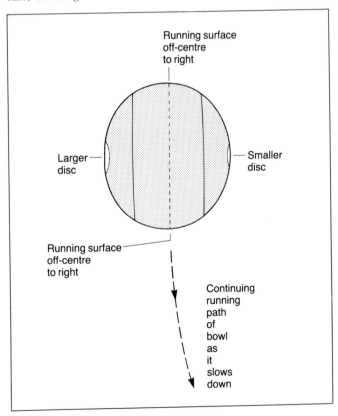

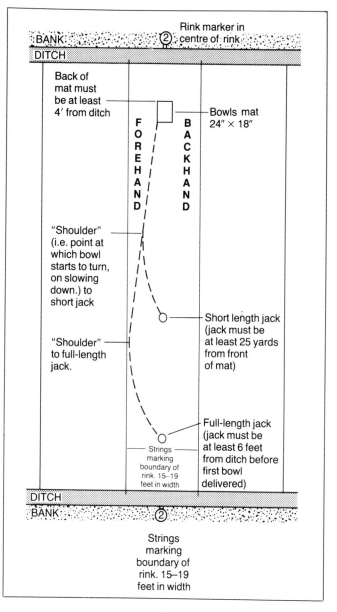

Rink marker in centre of rink

BANK

DITCH

Back of mat must be at least 4' from ditch

Bowls mat 24" × 18"

FOREHAND

BACKHAND

"Shoulder" (i.e. point at which bowl starts to turn, on slowing down.) to short jack

Short length jack (jack must be at least 25 yards from front of mat)

"Shoulder" to full-length jack.

Full-length jack (jack must be at least 6 feet from ditch before first bowl delivered)

Strings marking boundary of rink. 15–19 feet in width

DITCH

BANK

Strings marking boundary of rink. 15–19 feet in width

Forehand and backhand

The side of the rink on which the bowl is shown to be travelling in the diagram is the forehand. If the bowl was played on the other side of the rink it would be on the backhand.

In bowls, the terms forehand and backhand are the same as for the racquet sports. A right-handed player, playing on his right-hand side as he looked at the jack, would be playing on that forehand. On the left-hand side, it would be his backhand.

The small disc side of the bowl, ie the bias side, is always on the inside of the curve towards the jack.

Line and length

A bowl delivered in the correct direction, which finishes on the centre line of the rink, has been bowled on the right line.

A bowl delivered with the correct amount of impetus, or weight, so that it finishes at the same distance from the mat as the jack, has been bowled with the right length.

A bowl delivered on the right line with the right length is a perfectly-played bowl – it *is* a simple game! If he gets just two things right with every bowl, then a player will be playing perfect bowls. But no bowler will ever achieve perfection.

DELIVERY ACTIONS – SOME FAMOUS EXAMPLES

The two pictures (below left) of Willie Wood show part of the delivery action which seems to have acted as the role model for younger Scots players Richard Corsie, Hugh Duff and Andy Thomson. They all transfer their body weight quickly forward to such an extent that they give the appearance of running off the mat.

This action is appropriate for competing on the heavy greens in Scotland where Richard, Hugh and Andy all started playing at a young age. They needed the extra impetus for their growing bodies.

Picture 1 is of special interest. It shows Willie's thumb on top of the bowl. Although he had performed well on Australian greens (Commonwealth Gold in Brisbane in 1982), he has, subsequent to this photograph being taken, decided to move his thumb lower for better control on faster greens, both indoors and outdoors, in the southern hemisphere.

If any bulky bowler ever tells you that he bumps the bowl on delivery because he can't bend far enough, show him this picture of the finish of a delivery action. The 'Gentle Giant' with the sweet, silky-smooth, action is Bill Boettger (left) of Canada. His partner in several world-class events has been

fellow Canadian, Ron Jones. Ron is Liverpool-born and has the physique of a flat-race jockey, hence the inevitable nickname: 'Little and Large' when Ron and Bill appear on the green together. Bill's action is not only physically flawless, it contains good body language, with all movement positively forward along the delivery line.

There's no question here of his having to trim his action because of his physical frame, as viewers will have seen for themselves in the BBC coverage of the World Indoor Singles and Pairs.

25

THE SHOTS IN THE GAME

The main basic shots played in bowls are:

a The Draw Shot
b Resting Shot
c Resting-out Shot
d The Jack Trail
e Using a Bowl
f Follow-through, or Follow-on, Shot
g Fire, or Drive
h Block, or Stopper
i Position Bowl

The draw shot

The draw shot is the first one that a beginner must learn, and is the shot most used in bowls. The dotted lines in the diagram show the drawing line which might be required on the forehand and backhand of a rink.

In the use of the forehand, the line required is outside a bowl already played, and in the use of the backhand, inside a bowl already played. 'X' marks the spot where it is intended that the bowl will finish.

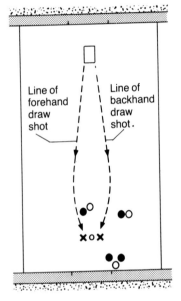

Line of forehand draw shot

Line of backhand draw shot.

Key

o Jack
O Bowls of bowler to play next—white
● Opposing bowls — black
x Intended finishing position of bowl.

26

Resting shot

The resting shot is played when another bowl, already played, is available for use as a drawing target. The diagram shows a position where a resting shot might be played.

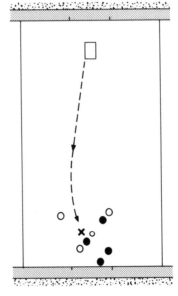

Resting-out shot

The resting-out shot differs from the resting shot in that it is played with sufficient impetus to knock an opposing bowl some distance away from the jack. The diagram shows a position where a resting-out shot would be attempted.

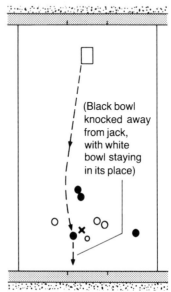

(Black bowl knocked away from jack, with white bowl staying in its place)

The jack trail

The diagram shows a good opportunity for 'white' to trail the jack to his own three waiting bowls.

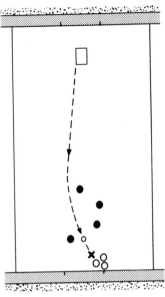

Using a bowl

In the diagram the 'white' player might try to 'use' one of his own bowls because both forehand and backhand are blocked for the draw shot, in that the opposing bowls are on the path which a draw shot would follow.

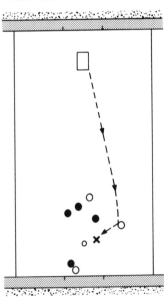

Follow-through, or follow-on, shot

In the position facing 'white', he may decide to play a follow-through, or follow-on, shot. He would be aiming to contact one of the opposing bowls with sufficient force to retain sufficient impetus to follow-through and finish close to the jack, but without so much weight that he travels too far past the jack.

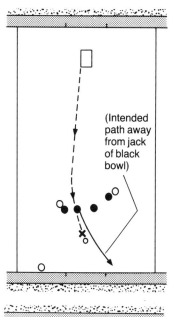

(Intended path away from jack of black bowl)

Fire, or drive

The position illustrated would call for a drive or fire by 'white'. The bowl is played with the maximum impetus the player can impart to it, without losing control of accuracy of line.

The prime target is for the jack to be forced through to the waiting bowls, but if slightly off the required line, the drive would remove opposing scoring bowls.

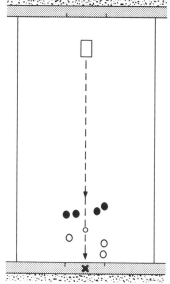

29

Block, or stopper

A block, or stopper, is played to prevent the opponent from playing on a specific route or line with his next bowl. In the diagram, 'white' is attempting to stop on the line his opponent would take if he were to drive. 'X' marks the spot where 'white' is trying to place his bowl.

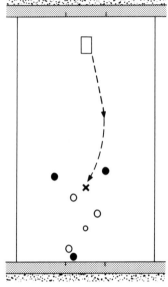

Position bowl

A position bowl is played to reduce the scoring possibilities for the opponent. In the diagram, 'white' is attempting to finish in position 'X' to stop his opponent scoring four shots with a jack-trailing shot on the forehand.

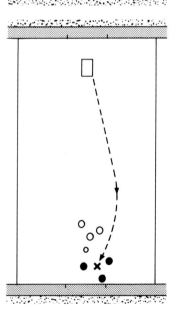

LEARNING FROM TELEVISION

Jimmy Davidson

Extensive BBC coverage of Indoor Bowls began in the early 1980s, when the World Pairs and UK Singles were added to the World Indoor Singles Championship, which was already transmitted from Coatbridge. As a direct result of the television coverage of these major events, participating players, viewing bowlers and rink officials have improved their personal standards of performance.

PARTICIPATING PLAYERS

I have, from time to time, needed to look again at tapes of events from the earlier years of television coverage. In sports such as athletics, where performance can be measured in time or distance, the rate of improvement can be precisely recorded. This measurement of sporting achievement seems to be especially important in the USA, where yards are gained on the football field, and the averages for all aspects of golf and the various strokes are systematically obtained and religiously recorded.

We have not, as yet, got to the stage in bowls where we could authoritatively say that the measured average distance from the jack to each bowl delivered by David Bryant in the 1987 Embassy Final against Tony Allcock was 'X' feet, 'Y' inches. I can, however, give you not only my own subjective assessment, based on re-examination of tapes over the years, that it was bowling of a higher standard than in any previous year, but I can also confidently assert that television bowling standards have improved, are improving and will improve further.

As a proud possessor of an early FA Coaching Certificate in the 'reign' of Walter Winterbottom, I could give many teaching sessions with groups of young players, all designed to improve their physical skills in the game. It could well be argued that a bowls player can learn all the basic physical skills he needs for his full bowling career in his *first* few sessions on the green.

However, the difference between a good bowler and a better bowler is usually, in my view, that the mental application of the winner was better than his opponent's on that particular day.

Since positive mental application is such an important factor in bowls played at any level, it becomes crucial under the pressures of playing before the eye of a television camera. To simply cope with this pressure is insufficient. A cocoon of concentration is essential. Once the level of concentration is sufficient enough, there is no room for any disruptive thoughts about the size of the audience at the venue or of being in front of television cameras. There are even some players who positively 'bask' in the warmth of television lights.

The concentration must not, however, be such a mental strain that it produces a physical reaction such as over-tension of key muscles in the arm. Insufficient physical impetus from the bowling arm is often due to tenseness caused by a psychological reaction to the pressure of a situation. The best players in all the target sports, of which bowls is one, learn to cultivate the sense and feeling of a concentrated mind in a relaxed body.

There was an impressive demonstration of the way in which fierce concentration can take away 'pressure' in a recent BBC *Body Matters* programme. An Olympic archer competed with people whose measured rate of heart beats increased as the camera turned on them. In the case of the Olympic archer, his heart beat actually reduced as he concentrated his mind and aimed fiercely on the gold centre of the target.

There are many factors which have contributed to improvement in the standard of concentration of bowlers in televised events. Television professionals have developed ways of producing their programmes without the cameras being too obtrusive. An example of this is the fact that, for the past two years, the BBC cameras positioned immediately behind the head and in the eye-line of the players on the mat, have been hidden behind a high-tech one-way glass screen.

Even the most idealistic bowls fan would have to admit that the increasing amount of prize money available has been a positive factor. After all, bigger prize money concentrates the mind so wonderfully well!

One major change made by both the British Isles and World

Indoor Bowls Councils can be shown to have improved the concentration of players as well as, in my view, providing better viewer entertainment. This is the introduction of the sets scoring system of a number of sets of seven shots, each replacing the traditional first to 21 shots.

David Bryant surprised me a couple of years after sets were first introduced. He said 'I'm not so sure about sets now Jim.' I was amazed because, at their introduction, David had been an enthusiastic supporter of the sets scoring system. All was explained when he added with a chuckle; 'They're all concentrating as well as me now!' Ask any experienced bowler and he'll tell you that by comparison he could 'go to sleep' in the middle of a 21-up game, where in sets there is the ever-present feeling that one loose end, or even one loose bowl, could lose them a set. Our own research showed that this view was accurate. We found that in 75 per cent of all ends of sets of seven shots played, the set could be won or lost on that end. There was an increase of potential climax which made viewing more compulsive. It also heightened the players' concentration. I heard one bowler express it in the terms of his profession as a teacher. He said that, in the same way as he was taught that pupils concentrated most in the first and last five minutes of a 40-minute lesson, he used to concentrate most at the beginning and the end of a 21-shot game. Now he couldn't get away with letting his concentration slip in the middle of a set game.

VIEWING BOWLERS

A bowler friend once told me that he always turned off the sound when I was commentating. He went on to reduce my sense of punctured pride when he added that he turned down the sound, whoever was commentating, once they'd finished the preliminaries of introducing the players and setting the scene. He explained that he liked to try to work out which shot he would select to play if he were in the place of the player with the next bowl, without being given any clues from the commentator. The words of advice given to me by the first experienced sports commentator for whom I acted as Bowls Summariser immediately sprang to mind. He told me that the main sports audience to whom I should address my comments were 'Fred and Freda from Scunthorpe, who had never played sport!'

The fact is, of course, that viewing bowlers learn most from watching the play of top bowlers – but if we commentators can also help a little ....

UMPIRES AND MARKERS

It is only natural that, as the raison d'être for televising bowls are the performances of the players in competition, the Umpires and Markers are only noticed when they make mistakes. At the last World Indoor Singles and Pairs, Tournament Director David Harrison introduced a Marker and Umpire Assessment Sheet which was completed by the competing players. Their assessments confirmed the view that the standards being achieved by the rink officials used in the Panel for television were of the highest order.

Having set that part of the record straight, let me also mention the two biggest fluffs made by television Bowls Markers. At one UK Singles event at Preston, the Marker did a 'John Williams'. John went down in television snooker history in an Alex Higgins game when he picked up the white ball instead of taking the pink from the pocket to re-pot it. Our Marker, equally mistakenly, picked up our white jack from the ditch and had to replace it hurriedly. On another occasion, on ITV, one of our Markers actually chalked the jack, instead of chalking the bowl which touched the jack. I won't tell you about the many occasions when commentators have wished that *their* minds had also gone blank – and that they had kept their mouths shut!

TELEVISION RECRUITMENT OF BEGINNERS

I wonder how many bowlers first took up the game after developing an interest through watching televised bowls. It must be a considerable number. I was told the true story of a London club whose membership was falling. They placed an advert in the local paper, inviting would-be members for instruction, with a view to joining the club. They paid for two insertions in the newspaper. The first insertion produced the pleasing response of 28 enquiries. Before the second advert appeared, a *Jack High* programme was transmitted by the BBC. The next week's postbag produced over 300 responses!

MAJOR BBC TELEVISION TOURNAMENTS 1987–1989

David Rhys Jones

THE WORLD INDOOR SINGLES CHAMPIONSHIP

A new home for the Embassy

World championship snooker was fired in a crucible – The Crucible – and the white heat produced there was fanned, and never extinguished. World championship bowls had its Crucible too. The arena which became synonymous with bowls was in an even more unlikely place than Sheffield. Coatbridge hosted the Embassy competition during its formative years, and its claustrophobic cockpit housed many a dramatic confrontation.

The final in 1979 between David Bryant and Ireland's legendary Jimmy Donnelly was the first of so many great matches. Bryant won the event for the first three years, then becoming a highly respected, and dangerous, ex-champion. Two Scots, John Watson and Bob Sutherland, delighted the home crowd with wins in 1982 and 1983, then a young Irishman, Jim Baker, beat an even younger player, Londoner Nigel Smith, in the 1984 final.

Terry Sullivan showed that Wales was not to be outdone when he defeated the Israeli, Cecil Bransky, in the final in 1985, after which the immaculate, blonde-haired Englishman, Tony Allcock, won the world title for two years in succession.

Duff reigns at Ally Pally

It was in 1988 that the world event was moved to a

David Rhys Jones

grand new home. London's

Alexandra Palace had housed one of the oldest indoor bowling clubs in England since 1909, but it had seen nothing like the uncanny consistency of Auchinleck's Hugh Duff.

Duff, aged 23, had given warning of his potential the previous year, when he had got as far as the semi-final, but the way in which he swept aside such mighty challengers as Jim Baker, Willie Wood, David Bryant and Wynne Richards took everyone by surprise.

Hugh certainly 'duffed' up his opponents, losing only two sets in the championship. Not even Bryant was able to find a way to sabotage the Scot's brilliant drawing, and he was beaten in straight sets in the semi-final. A journalist in the Ally Pally Press Room searching, as ever, for a catchy phrase, came up with an idea for a punchy headline. 'Duff chuffed – Bryant stuffed,' he suggested. It rang true, but we were all too polite to use it!

In the final, the Auchinleck star faced Wynne Richards – the Welshman who plays for England. Wynne had just returned from Auckland where he had earned two bronze medals and had helped England to win the team gold in the World Championships. He had also outplayed the holder, Allcock, in the semi-final. It was no contest. On the very last end, Richards drew three bowls to within 15 inches of the jack. Duff put all his within a foot. As his last, despairing draw just failed to save, Wynne held out his hand to Hugh, and said, 'Brilliant son, absolutely b-b-brilliant!' We were all inclined to agree.

Corsie delivers first class at Preston Guild Hall

That was that, as far as Alexandra Palace was concerned. The following year saw the Embassy world circus pitch its tent in the reliable Preston Guild Hall, scene of so many CIS UK Singles Championships.

More surprises were in store. Those who thought that Duff had set a record that would last for years were in for a shock. Another young Scotsman, Richard Corsie, aged 22, became the youngest man to win a world bowls title indoors or out, when he completely outplayed his boyhood hero, Willie Wood, in the final.

Jubilation as Hugh Duff wins the World Championship 1988

Richard Corsie, winner of the 1989 World Championship

Before the final started, Willie told BBC presenter, David Icke, how Richard used to come into the Edinburgh stadium and sit for hours at the rink-side watching him play. During the final, it was Willie who was forced to be the spectator as Richard, a postman, made a succession of first class deliveries.

Although he did not drop a set in his semi or final, Richard's path to the title was not a smooth one. In the first two rounds, he struggled to beat top New Zealanders, Rowan Brassey, whose forebears were Scottish, and Ivan Bottica, who was born in Yugoslavia. Both matches were to five sets, with Richard having to win the last two sets each time.

Then, in the quarter final, Richard faced 19-year-old Hong Kong hopeful, Mark McMahon, who was born in Fife. One of the most popular players of the event, both on and off the green, Mark wore his heart on his sleeve and played with a natural, naive skill although he had no answer for Richard's brilliant all-round game.

While Duff had won in 1988 with a devastating display of drawing, Corsie, whose drawing was delightful, also fired superbly. He ditched the jack with a thunderbolt three times in the final, and each time his cannon-ball finished snugly alongside the jack. Powerful, accurate, exciting and perhaps a little fortunate. Supremely entertaining, too.

David Bryant, who had fallen to Bottica in the first round, watched the final on television, and assessed Corsie's performance as the best he had ever seen. 'That's a real compliment, coming from him,' said Corsie, who collected the winner's cheque for £18,000 – the biggest-ever prize in the history of the game.

Exactly ten years before, when Bryant defeated Donnelly, he had won nothing at all, even though television cameras were there to record the action. Bowls has come a long way in a relatively short period of time.

UK Indoor championship

Unlike the Embassy, the CIS UK Singles Championship has always been played on the portable rink, and always in the splendid Preston Guild Hall.

Many say that it is harder to win the UK title than the world event for, no matter how strong the overseas contingent may be, they are generally inexperienced in the indoor game and are suffering somewhat from jet-lag.

Britain is the home of indoor bowls and, with 32 of the top UK players in the field, it is not surprising that the event is rated so highly. There have been some memorable finals since the first in 1983, when David Bryant turned on what may have been his finest ever performance to beat the reigning world indoor champion, Bob Sutherland, in straight sets.

The following year saw the emergence of Terry Sullivan, who edged home against rising star, Tony Allcock in a final that was watched by over seven million viewers, and which placed televised bowls firmly on the programme planners' agenda.

1985 was Jim Baker's year. Still in his twenties, this young Irishman had already won the World Outdoor Fours and the World Indoor Singles. He went through his varied repertoire of shots which distinguish him as a complete bowler. John Watson, 1982 world champion, was the man Baker defeated in the final.

In 1986 Steve Rees and David Bryant gave us perhaps the

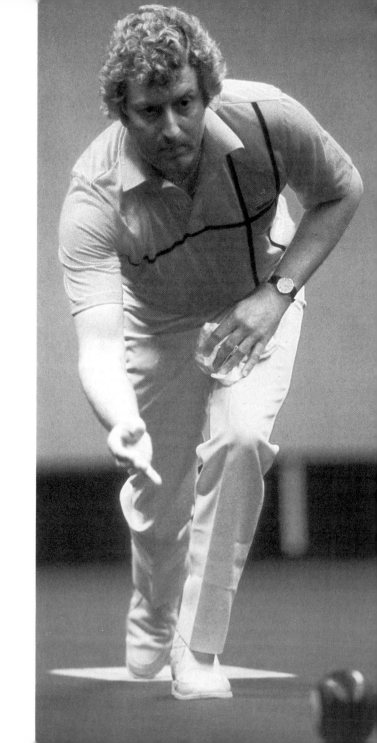

Above: Bryant v Rees. 'How do I get out of this?'
Left: Tony Allcock

most remarkable game ever witnessed on television. Rees won
the first four sets of a nine-set final, and dominated to the tune
of 28 shots to nine. There appeared to be no way back for
Bryant. The pipe-smoking Maestro from Clevedon made the
bravest fight back, however, winning the next four sets to square
the match. But justice was done when the 26-year-old Rees took
the ninth and deciding set to clinch the title.

Allcock – at last!

By the time the CIS came round again in 1987, Tony Allcock
had won two World Singles titles, and was clearly keen to con-
firm his status as the new Number One. He did so, winning the
UK title for the first time, although he scraped through in the
final against the Irish Pink Panther, David Corkill.

Tony's path to the final brought him up against three top Scots – Hugh Duff, Angus Blair and Willie Wood – and the semi-final against Willie produced some of the most exciting bowling ever seen on television.

Although his opponents played well, Allcock seemed to have the answer to every problem. The Gloucestershire star breaks just about every rule in the coaching manual, but gets away with it! His curious, unorthodox 'flick' delivery, and brave (some would say foolhardy) choice of running shots, are hardly calculated to produce consistently good bowls.

The proof of the play, however, is in the results and Tony, indoors and out, has a record that confounds his armchair critics. The secret lies in his supreme confidence – and his totally natural ability. With his flair, there is little need for technique and with his unerring strike rate, there is no call for caution when it comes to choosing the right shot to play.

A man called Smith

A young man called Nigel Smith shot to prominence in 1984 when he reached the World Singles final. Another Smith, Gary, with lots of the same brand of London confidence and a similar accent, took the Preston Guild Hall by storm in 1988. Gary, an administrative assistant bank manager from Kent, was only 28, but had been bowling at a high level since he won his county singles title in his teens. Overshadowed to some extent by the arrival of Andy Thomson and his Cyphers indoor club, he relished his first singles championship on the portable rink.

Taking a leaf out of the Allcock book, Gary based his winning style on drawing to the jack, but was never afraid to use the running wood – one of the most difficult shots in the game. His success rate was phenomenal. Often outdrawn, he escaped from hopeless positions using accurate attacking bowls.

In the final, Richard Corsie must have wondered what he had to do to keep the shots that he painstakingly piled around the jack. Although we didn't know it at the time, Corsie was building up for his Embassy win a few months later, and was running into form. But he could do nothing against the inspired Smith.

Gary Smith

The following morning, back on his postman's round in Edinburgh, salt was rubbed into Corsie's wounds. The first customer to sign for a registered parcel was – Gary Smith. Not the same one, of course, but Richard would like to take this opportunity of apologising if his doorstep manner left something to be desired!

Gary was a gift for the cameras. All too often, pressure and concentration turn top bowlers into grim, deadpan adversaries. Smith broke the mould, unashamedly wearing his heart on his sleeve. His face was a picture, worth many a close-up. He grimaced when things went wrong, smiled when they went right, and punched the air when he was delighted.

When the two finalists came to the after-match interview, they behaved splendidly. Both in their twenties, they were a credit to the great tradition of bowls. Corsie was sportsmanlike in defeat and Smith, for all his seemingly arrogant victory salutes, was a gracious winner.

Bryant, 'the Maestro' is back with a bang

'The man you have to beat.' Most world-class players would admit that when David Bryant is playing, the above statement is true. In 1979 he won the first World Indoor Championship and followed up the next two years, before handing over to the younger contingent.

It was to become a similar story in the CIS UK Indoor Singles when 'the maestro' won the first UK title in 1983. Again, the younger element took over – until 1989. This time, David Bryant was determined to prove that he was more than just the respected ex-champion. With some astounding performances, he won back the UK title, pulling the occasional rabbit out of the top hat.

Right from the first round match, it was obvious that David was raring to go. Bill Hobart from Boston in Lincolnshire, who was on his UK debut, was 'the maestro's' first victim. It could be said that Bill was unlucky, but then the sheer brilliance of Bryant's final wood with shot against him and the score at 1–1 in sets and 6–6 in the final set was a joy to watch. Very few players could produce a shot like that under pressure. The 'old man of bowls' (not meant with any disrespect) was on his way up again.

The next round saw the young pretender and holder, Gary Smith, going out of the championship, beaten 3–1 by Angus Blair.

The biggest surprise of the tournament came when the current World Indoor Singles Champion, Richard Corsie, was slaughtered by his Scots team-mate and 1987 World Indoor Champion, Hugh Duff. The score was an embarrassing 7–1, 7–5, 7–1.

So what was David Bryant going to do against his old rival Jim Baker? Once again, Bryant's steely temperament enabled him to demonstrate what a great fighter he is – 2–1 sets up, 6–6 in the fourth and another one out of the hat!

One of the best indoor bowls matches ever seen on television was played in this round. The Ladies' World Indoors Singles Champion, Margaret Johnston from Londonderry in Northern Ireland, had the misfortune to be drawn against the world's number one singles player, Tony Allcock. The fact that it was the first time ladies were invited to appear on level terms with men in a flat green major television championship didn't seem to worry the Irish housewife as much as people expected.

She won the first set 7–6 in a very tight game. Tony then took the second set reasonably easily 7–2 but had to bring out his best in the third to just win 7–6. Margaret, sensing she had Tony worried, played beautifully to win the fourth set 7–4. And then came that fifth and final set which was so full of drama and excitement. 6–6 and Mary, well placed, played a very loose bowl. Although the fifth set had been going away from him, Tony Allcock suddenly had the chance to win the match. He took it with a perfect draw to win the set 7–6 and to go into the next round. The full house at the Preston Guild Hall gave the Irish lady a tremendous reception and poor Tony looked absolutely drained. What a good match!

David Bryant soldiered on and had good wins over Neil McGhee and Stephen Rees to reach the final. Tony Allcock disposed of Hugh Duff and was then bowled out by an impressive-looking David Corkill.

So to the final between David Bryant and David Corkill. With all the brilliant bowling seen earlier, everyone was reluctant to hope for a barnstorming final. But it happened!

'The maestro' seemed strangely complacent as the final started, whilst David Corkill, the bowling machine, took advantage of an unusually uneasy David Bryant. He went into a 2–0 lead and when he went ahead 6–3 in the third set, the whole of the Guild Hall were feeling saddened. David Corkill was bowling brilliantly, but Bryant seemed to suddenly break out of his lethargy and began to fight back.

He won the third set 7–6 and then the fourth, to make it two sets each. Then, in the fifth and deciding set, they both turned the power on. 6–6, Corkill lying two shots for the title, Bryant with his final bowl. He pulled his third 'rabbit' out of the hat as, with another brilliant draw shot, he took both of David Corkill's shot woods out, regaining the title he won six years earlier.

What a wonderful week of bowling, and who could have forecast such a magnificent game of bowls in the final by two of the most outstanding exponents of the sport.

WORLD INDOOR PAIRS CHAMPIONSHIP – NEW VENUE, NEW SPONSOR, NEW FORMAT

The third Midland Bank World Indoor Pairs Championship took place in the plush setting of the Bournemouth International Centre, where David Bryant and Tony Allcock had combined superbly to win the event twice. It was surprising enough that they had loosened their hold on the championship, but a major shock that the spoils were snaffled by a couple of swashbuckling Australian swagmen – Jim Yates and Ian Schuback.

Yates played consistent, orthodox bowls, drawing beautifully to the jack with monotonous regularity, and giving his skip a dream start, end after end. Schuback took full advantage, and looked by far the most professional overseas visitor to appear in any televised event. He had, after all, been a professional tennis coach and, on his only previous visit to these shores, had collected the silver medal at the 1986 Commonwealth Games. His fine personal performance was augmented with a degree of showmanship that went down well with the spectators as well as with television audiences.

Bryant and Allcock were beaten by Gary Smith and Andy

Margaret Johnston

Thomson in the semi-final, but the Kent pair were never in with a chance in the final, which was well and truly dominated from start to finish by the Aussie pair, who won by five sets to one.

'Fair dinkum!' exclaimed the Coolangata skip as he chuckled his way through the Press conference that followed the final. 'Would you say that winning this event was the highlight of your bowling career?' he was asked. 'No,' he replied 'It's the highlight of my life!'

The World Pairs moved to the Preston Guild Hall in 1989, sharing the spotlight and the portable rink with the singles. In spite of some concern over how the two events, both now sponsored by Embassy, would fit together, the pairs did not seem to suffer by comparison with the singles, and bowling was of a very high standard.

David Bryant and Tony Allcock won the championship for the third time in four attempts, beating Rowan Brassey and Peter Belliss in straight sets in a one-sided final. It was sweet enough revenge for the English pair, who had been beaten by the Kiwis in the final of the World Outdoor Pairs championship at Auckland in 1988. They took semi-final revenge too, over the Kent pair, Smith and Thomson, who had ousted them at the same stage last time.

Defending champions, Jim Yates and Ian Schuback, were surprised in the first round by Roy Cutts and Wynne Richards, who were immediatly eliminated by their English team-mates, Smyth and Halmai. Smyth and Halmai were beaten by Brassey and Belliss, so when the New Zealanders were thrashed by Bryant and Allcock in the final the holders were, on paper, the weakest team in the competition!

During the lead-up to the final, it was the confident Allcock who produced the magic. In the early rounds, Bryant appeared to be sadly out of touch. Against Brassey, however, it was a different story. Bryant was in one of his most determined moods, making Allcock's task much easier.

David Bryant in action

49

WHAT A LOAD OF BOWLS

Gary Smith

I remember well the first problem head to which I had to bowl at the age of about six or seven. Could I get my orange marble through a small gap between a red and green marble to displace my arch rival's blue marble and win the street title? It was already evident to my parents that, not only had I inherited my father's love of the game of bowls, but also that the will and motivation to win would always form a major part of my character.

Over the next few years, I travelled with my father (a well-respected Kent player) watching almost every game he played. I remember the frustration I felt at not being able to play on the greens, many of which had an age limit of 16. My early practice required me to find any adjacent grassy strip where I could use a set of four cricket balls, together with a snooker cue ball for a jack. Whenever I dared venture onto a bowling green there was always a park keeper hiding behind an adjacent bush like a Japanese sniper, ready to chase me off with a patronising comment. When I look back, I wonder just how I managed to achieve the dizzy academic heights of four 'A' levels and ten 'O' levels when most of my studying and homework was done around the edge of a bowling green.

Despite the fact that I played football, tennis and cricket for the school, none of these held the same fascination as bowls, even though it had an 'old man's game' image amongst my closest friends.

Over the past 15 years of playing, nothing has given me greater pleasure than seeing the expansion in the popularity of the game, especially amongst the younger fraternity, despite the initial resistance to such developments by some of the old guard. We should remember that it was 'the maestro' himself, David Bryant CBE, who was quoted as saying, 'Bowls is a young man's game that older people can play.' Another favourite saying of mine, which refers to the resistance shown by some older players

Wynne Richards with Hugh Duff at the Embassy World Indoor
Championships (1988)

to being replaced as a skip by a younger up and coming player is
'Those players who say leads should stay as leads, are skips who
wish to stay as skips.'

The sport has become richer in talent and entertainment
value since more competitive tournaments aimed at under 25s,
under 16s and under 12s have been introduced by the national
bodies. One only has to look at the ages of two recent World
Indoor Singles champions, Hugh Duff and Richard Corsie, both
in their early to mid-twenties, to see the ability of these young
bowlers. At 31, I am probably considered to be a veteran!

The governing bodies themselves have also moved with the
times to the point that the once feared, and most definitely
unwanted, professional or semi-professional player is now wel-
comed alongside the ordinary club player. They have shown an
exhilarating degree of professionalism, and are to be congratu-
lated for the way in which they have handled the game's progress
to today's position where bowls receives increased television
exposure together with its attendant sponsorship.

Despite these dramatic changes, sportsmanship remains supreme amongst participants and spectators. Competition may be fierce, but the etiquette of the game is always honoured, which is why bowls has such a good name. Long may this continue.

At this stage, I must comment on the encouragement and assistance I received in my early years of competitive bowling from a number of individuals. Firstly, my father, who sadly is no longer with us. I had the pleasure of watching my first indoor international at Folkestone in 1984, when I was picked to play two in a rink skipped by David Bryant, my father's hero. My father died one month later, but I am sure he is watching from above whenever I play. I now use his woods so perhaps there has been some heavenly guidance over the last few years. My mother remains my greatest fan. She gave up the title of 'bowls widow' some years ago to play herself. 'If you can't beat them join them' is her favourite motto.

My greatest thanks must go to a real Kent and England star, Maurice Phillips, now better known as a first class coach and umpire. I played with Maurice for many years and I can safely say that he taught me almost everything I know. His sharp mind, coupled with his technical ability, brought us both many titles and gave me the grounding for a successful future in the game.

Another early partner was England international Bob Harris, who died at a tragically young age. Bob was a first class, aggressive skip, from whom I learnt a lot of my skipping skills. Bob was never the most subtle of opponents. One amusing incident springs to mind when in a dispute over a measure at the Bournemouth tournament, he upset an elderly gentleman, some 30 years his senior. The dispute ended up with the aged gentleman dropping a bowl on Bob's foot, disabling him for the rest of the game.

Humour and good fun have always been a feature during my years in the game, and I hope that readers will smile at some of the following recollections none of which, I hope, will offend anyone.

A famous story from my county of Kent involved a gentleman with a false leg, who was playing in a pairs match. This disability was unknown to the opposing skip as there were no obvious signs of his disability. On one particular end, the bowler with the false leg had bowled his bowls, walked to the other end of the green, and stood with his false leg on the green and his other leg in the ditch. The opposing skip decided to fire at the head but missed completely, striking the disabled player's false leg at great speed. The impact completely removed the bottom part of the false leg which flew up in the air, and the poor fellow fell over on to the bank. Obviously this caused great concern amongst the other players on the green and everyone rushed to his assistance – bar one person. When they looked for the skip who had delivered the blow, he was found to be prostrate at the other end of the green, having fainted at the thought of the damage he had done. Let me hasten to add that both players were perfectly all right afterwards.

Another very memorable incident occurred when John Bell and I were selected to represent England in the Hong Kong International Classic Pairs in 1983. If ever a man missed his true vocation in life surely it is John Bell, who I am sure could have been a great comedy star. Anyway, linking this tale to the previous anecdote, Ireland's skip in the competition, Paul Smyth, an excellent player who, despite having a false leg, plays at the highest international level. Over the two and a half weeks in Hong Kong, poor Paul had a series of mishaps, the worst being when a rivet sheared in his false leg. Our only indication of the mishap was the sight of a leg being passed over the tops of heads in a crowded function room on its way to a local welder. Fortunately Paul had a spare leg with him.

The next incident occurred at a newly-opened athletics stadium, where John found a true friend in the form of the biggest cricket in Hong Kong. It was John Bell who first saw the creature. He prodded it with his clog, causing it to take

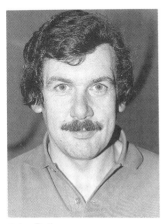

John Bell

53

off from its praying mantis position on the track. It quickly attached itself to the side of Paul Smyth's face. Paul, reacting as quickly as ever – ie after approximately two minutes – brushed it aside. It flew off, only to return and attach itself to Paul's more delicate parts! John Bell laughed about that incident continually for the next 24 hours, and he and Paul have had a love-hate relationship ever since. The cry of 'I hate yer Bell' cried in a Dublin accent has been heard at many an International series since.

Returning to the game itself, I must say that nothing can beat the atmosphere of the Home International series, with all the national pride it engenders. Despite the fierce competition on the green, many friendships have been formed amongst the players from all countries. The professionalism shown by the England selectors and officials, as well as by the players, has made England the best team in the British Isles and it is a pleasure to be involved in what has become almost a family set-up.

Undoubtedly, the experience of obtaining 36 England caps, coupled with the good grounding I received early on, as well as the company with whom I play, have been vital in the build-up to my greatest achievements – the England and UK Singles titles, as well as reaching the final of the World Pairs and semi-final in the World Singles.

My partnership with Andy (Bagpipes) Thomson is a combination which has over the years grown in strength to the point where, despite our own distinctive, individual talents and records, our names are invariably linked. Andy is the greatest player with whom I have played, ranking overall with David Bryant and Tony Allcock. In my opinion, his major strengths are his determination and good leadership, as well as his obvious technical ability. Over the years, he has been both my greatest rival and my ally and we have driven each other on to increasing levels of achievement. We were both overwhelmed by the honour recently bestowed upon us when we were selected to represent England in the Commonwealth Games Pairs in New Zealand.

Martyn Selejer and Terry Heppell have teamed up with Andy and myself to form the most successful club four in history. Playing with such talented players has been a major reason for my own individual skills and I take this opportunity to thank them most sincerely. I would also like to thank the clubs with whom I have achieved my successes, namely Forest Hill, Old Colferans, Blackheath and Greenwich and Cyphers together with the officers and members, as well as my county of Kent and its selectors.

In looking at the future, I feel that the game has nothing but success ahead of it. However, it is vital that bowls is kept at the forefront of television output. Talks of a cutback are disturbing, especially during a spell of such increased popularity. Bowls appeals to old and young alike, and for that reason, should be popular with sponsors. However, the game does need characters with distinctive personalities with which viewers can identify. There are still too many men in the street who only know David Bryant or Tony Allcock.

Television is an entertainment media, and that is what we players must endeavour to provide with, perhaps, a greater degree of razzamatazz to liven up the image of the game. Satellite television and greater expansion in America and Europe may provide exciting new challenges to the game and its players. To keep bowls heading on the correct course, I am convinced that the professional ranks will have to be swelled. Too many top international players find that they have increasing problems in maintaining a balance between their employment and family commitments and the expanding bowls diary. Whilst I receive tremendous encouragement from my employers Barclays Bank plc, I know that others do not get the same support.

I would like to sum up by setting out the elements which, I feel, have contributed towards my success in bowls. I hope that the information will assist up and coming players. Firstly, watch good players and learn from the type of shots they play. By studying them you will also learn a lot about developing the correct temperament and psychology which is so important in our sport. Ensure that your basic techniques of delivery and stance are correct, referring to your local qualified coach for guidance, if necessary. Coaching schemes have improved tremendously over recent years, mainly due to the major influence of Jimmy Davidson. Be sure you know the rules. There is nothing worse than being cheated out of shots due to lack of knowledge. Take every opportunity to play with and against good players in a competitive environment. Only through experience will you develop the all-round skills required to get to the very top.

More Stars of the Flat Game

Keith Phillips

David Corkill

David Corkill had one special advantage in his quest to achieve high Irish international bowling honours – his father, David senior, is the top bowling coach in the province. David senior, in the first year of the British Association of National Coaches Awards, was a recipient of one of their prestigious awards. Born in 1960 in Belfast, David Corkill was first taught how to play by his father at the tender age of 10. But there were problems. As David puts it, his introduction to the game 'seemed to cause a certain amount of concern for some of the older members of my father's club.' So David was only allowed to play at the short-mat indoor club before other members arrived, or during intervals between games.

He had a phased introduction to the outdoor game. His father insisted that he 'groove-in' his delivery action on a grass verge beside the green before he was allowed on to the green itself. That delivery action is now possibly the most distinctive in top level bowls. It has commentators searching for characterisations and similes. Perhaps the most used cliché has been 'stalking his bowl like a panther'. One ITV 'fun-clip' which greatly amused David featured his action accompanied by the theme music from the *Pink Panther* cartoons.

On a more serious level, David Corkill and Jim Baker have been streets ahead of their fellow bowlers from Ireland in international competition. David beat Jim in the 1986 final of ITV's *Superbowl*, but Jim has achieved both legs of what is still David's principal remaining bowls ambition – to win an outdoor or indoor World title – Jim has achieved both, including the Embassy World Indoor Singles in 1984.

David Corkill

But David's closest bowling encounter, and it couldn't have been closer, was with Irish bowler, Margaret Johnston in October 1988 in the ITV *Superbowl* final. The score by which David squeaked home was a score that sounds scripted – 7–6, 6–7, 6–7, 7–6, 7–6. The atmosphere of this match resembled the nail-biting tension of the Dennis Taylor versus Steve Davis World Snooker Final – David revels in it.

He earned his first international cap at the ripe old age of 18 years, and after 20 years of bowling, 12 of them at senior level, he still feels he hasn't reached his peak. I'm sure his world title will come in the near future.

RICHARD CORSIE

Richard was born in Edinburgh in 1966. He was considered eccentric when, at the age of 12, he started playing bowls instead of football like all the other kids. He won a junior title at 14 and held senior Scottish and British titles at the age of 16. He was immediately selected for Scotland, which can only be a record, and he was the only person to hold Scottish junior indoor and outdoor titles.

His job as a postman enables him to practise in the afternoons. He starts work at 4 am, finishes at 12.30 pm and then plays for two hours every day. He is allowed to take leave without pay to compete in major tournaments, but does not get any special privileges. Therefore, in order to make up his wages, he has to win, and winning competitions overseas has given him the most satisfaction.

He lost to Gary Smith in the 1988 UK Singles, but was the youngest player to get to the semi-finals of the same tournament three years ago. Young players have a professional approach to bowls, unlike the older players who have tended to treat it like a part-time game. Richard would give up his job tomorrow if there were enough televised tournaments, by which he could earn a decent living.

One evening last March, the 23-year-old postman used a Scottish pound note to pay for a drink at the bar of the Indoor Club where he plays at Milton Street in Edinburgh. An old bowler sitting at the other end of the bar commented 'Now you've only got £17,999 left Richard son!' He was referring to Richard's

Richard Corsie

winning the Embassy World Indoor Singles Championship at Preston Guild Hall that month, when he collected £18,000 – so far the biggest amount of winner's prize money to be won at any bowls event in the history of the sport.

For many viewers, two images of that televised success (in which Richard became the youngest-ever World Singles Champion) will persist. The first image might be that of Richard 'whitewashing' one of his own bowling idols, 50-year-old Willie Wood, by five sets to love in the final. The evening session of just one set, watched by a packed house, finished 7–0 in just 18 minutes.

The second vivid feature of the final was a handful of viciously accurate, successful drives by Richard. Viewers might have been surprised to learn that the biggest influence in Richard's bowling career was a Scottish international lead, John Summers. As a schoolboy, Richard marvelled at the immaculate, gentle, drawing accuracy of John, who led for Scotland in the 1980 World Outdoor Championships in Australia and who collected silver medals in the Triples and Fours.

Richard is quoted thus: 'I have this reputation as an aggressive player and I know that, in the early days, I perhaps fired indiscriminately, but if John taught me anything, it was the value of drawing to the jack. It's the basic shot in the game, and while the drive is useful in moderation, you must be able to draw, draw and draw.' Richard's drawing ability has won him international caps, both indoor and outdoor.

Richard will be representing Scotland again in the Commonwealth Games at Auckland, New Zealand, in 1990. He will be hoping to improve on the bronze he collected at the Games in 1986 in his home town, and to match the singles gold medal collected by Willie Wood in Brisbane, Australia, in 1982.

HUGH DUFF
Hugh was born in Rankiston, Ayrshire, in 1963 and first played bowls at the age of 17, yet anther convert from football. He played for Auchinleck indoor club with Scottish international Andy Faulkner and was picked for international honours at the age of 20. He is one of the few bowlers who was brought up with the indoor game and only started playing the outdoor game at top level in 1988.

He is also one of the few professionals in the sport and, at the age of 26, the youngest. Early in his career he trained very hard for four hours a day, and it paid off in 1988 when he won the World Singles title at Alexandra Palace, beating Wynne Richards in the final.

Wynne must have thought he had done the hard part of the

Hugh Duff

job when be beat Tony Allcock in the semi-final. After all, Tony had looked on course for a hat-trick as the 1986 and 1987 champion. But Hugh was waiting for him in the final, and Wynne must have felt shell-shocked when he lost the first two sets 0–7, 1–7, before losing by five sets to one.

The scores in the first two sets had a vaguely familiar ring to them and this was confirmed from the commentary box during the television transmission. In the 1987 semi-final against David Bryant, Hugh lost the first two sets 1–7, 0–7 before losing narrowly by two sets to three. One of the ends of that semi-final had

61

David Rhys Jones and Jimmy Davidson positively 'purring' in the Coatbridge commentary box. They both still describe the end which finished with Hugh drawing round a pile of seven bowls to within a fraction of an inch of the jack, as the best finale they have ever seen.

Hugh's game is, perhaps more than any other world-class bowler, particularly reliant on the pure draw shot. He does, when forced to do so, use the running bowl, but is clearly happiest when drawing. So much so that in the post-final interview at Alexandra Palace, the appropriate query to Hugh from David Icke was 'where did you learn to draw like that?' As usual, the essential point of Hugh's answer was a somewhat self-deprecating smile and a faint blush.

Hugh has the same manager – Ian Doyle – as snooker player Stephen Hendry, and Jimmy Davidson has helped him in his rise to stardom. He also follows the fortunes of Willie Wood to learn more. Having won the World Singles title, Hugh's ambition now is to keep playing at international level and to keep winning titles. He is, in fact, dedicated to bowls and, with the game so much a part of his life, it is hardly surprising that Hugh married the girl who was the youngest-ever Ayrshire Singles Champion at the age of 21. They were married at that famous wedding place, Gretna Green, on 2 October 1987. Hugh must have a forgiving nature. The first bowls final he ever lost was to 15-year-old Helen some six years before!

IAN SCHUBACK

Ian was born in Victoria Sale, Australia, in 1952 and is married with two daughters, Kim and Danielle. He started his career as a tennis player at the age of eight or nine and, at the age of 20, became one of the youngest ever tennis coaches in Australia. Ian was offered a lucrative contract in West Germany to coach tennis, which he turned down. He now regrets saying 'no', putting his decision down to immaturity. He took up rules football, moved to Melbourne to play tennis again, then went back to football. However he put paid to his football career when he broke his jaw.

Ian Schuback at the Midland Bank World Pairs Bowls (1988)

Ian Schuback started to play bowls after watching on Australian television, the crowd-pleasing performance of an English bowler in the 1980 World Championship at Frankston, Australia. He had previously thought that the sport was a bit staid but, having been entertained as a viewer, he thought he would 'give it a go'.

Ian won 50 titles in the first seven years of his professional bowling career. In December 1987, at Bournemouth, he won the World Indoor Pairs Championship with his partner Jim Yates. One of the BBC commentary team covering the event was Mal Hughes – the English bowler who had tempted Ian into taking up the game seven years earlier.

Mal had won a special award as the Personality of the 1980 World Championship, and something in the way he played bowls has definitely rubbed off on Ian. One programme biography on him stated 'In December 1987 the viewing public discovered a new hero, someone who played the serious game of bowls with distinct relish.'

Jim Yates and Ian Schuback made bowling history with that World Pairs Championship as the first overseas players ever to win a World Indoor title. Overseas players normally find it difficult to adapt to indoor conditions but, as the indoor version of the sport expands overseas, players will become more versatile.

37-year-old Ian practises at the Tweed Heads Club, a superb bowls complex in Australia, with an indoor green that David Bryant describes as one of the best bowling surfaces in the world. He is now the Secretary/Manager of the Hills Bowling Club in Sydney, New South Wales, and would seem to have as bright a bowling future as any bowler in the nation. Australia has almost 450,000 registered men and women bowlers, compared with the second biggest, England, which has approximately 130,000 men and 45,000 women who play on outdoor flat greens.

Ian gives himself another three years in the game, during which time his aim is to win the World Indoor and Outdoor titles and to play in the 1990 Commonwealth Games. After that his time will be devoted to his family and his real-estate business. In his opinion, bowls is changing, becoming more like tennis – base-line shots to power shots played by young fearless bowlers, like Mike MacMahon (Hong Kong), Cameron Curtis (Australia) and Richard Corsie (Scotland).

PRESENTING BOWLS ON TELEVISION

David Icke

Within minutes of arriving at Preston for my first BBC bowls event, I was left in no doubt of one thing: Bowls is fun. I realised this as soon as I met a rather portly Scot called Jim Barclay, then one of the markers at the UK Indoor Championship. He shoots jokes at you like an out-of-control machine gun.

'Did you hear the one about the man who put his arm in a tank of piranha fish and they didn't attack him? He had a tattoo saying "Rangers for the Cup" – and not even piranha fish would swallow that.' Or, 'Did you hear about (a Scottish bowls official) who was arrested by the police in the bar last night? He was charged with breaking into a pound, but they dropped the charges when they heard it was a first offence.' Or, 'Did you hear about the Scotsman who found an Australian penny and emigrated?' One after the other they come and from time to time some are even funny!

For many years the bowlers had been looking for a way of turning the joke on Jim, and in my first BBC tournament he handed it to them lock, stock and barrel. Near the end of the first afternoon, the jack ended up in the ditch and the officials decided on a measure to settle the end. All except Jim, that is. For some reason he forgot what he was doing and picked up the jack! His face was a picture as it dawned on him what he'd done. He quickly tried to put it back before anyone noticed. As it was live on BBC2 at the time,

David Icke

65

that was pretty optimistic to say the least. Anyway, the players were very good about it and they agreed to accept the point where Jim thought the jack had been.

After the game, a plan was hatched between the players, officials and the BBC to pull his leg. The Tournament Director, David Harrison, told Jim that there had been a lot of complaints to the BBC switchboard and that viewers were demanding that he answer for his conduct. He was told that the BBC wanted to interview him live before the start of the evening session about this incident which had 'caused a storm of protest from viewers.' For the good name of bowls, he would have to put his side of the story.

I was waiting on the rink with all the cameras in place when Jim arrived in his official uniform of blue jacket and white trousers. His trousers, in fact, matched the colour of his face. 'They are coming to us very shortly,' I said, even though there wasn't another programme for hours and the only people watching the interview were the players who were viewing it on the closed circuit television in their lounge.

'Welcome back to Preston,' I said, 'where we are going to talk to the man at the centre of a major storm which has erupted here today. He's Jim Barclay, who picked up a live jack from the ditch this afternoon before a measure could take place,' etc. etc. Jim's face got whiter and his eyes stared at the floor.

'Now, Jim Barclay,' I asked, 'what actually happened?' He began his earnest explanation of the incident, while I was almost biting my tongue in an effort not to laugh. The harder I tried, the tougher I was with Jim, in a desperate bid to keep a straight face. 'But come on, Mr Barclay, this is a terribly serious incident isn't it?' 'Oh yes,' agreed Jim, his head getting lower with every passing second, 'it is very serious.'

This went on for some five minutes or more and by the end of the interview the players were in hysterics. Then, with Jim not knowing where his next word was coming from, I said that the incident was so bad that we had to get the opinions of his fellow officials. On to the rink they came, on a prearranged cue, bearing a special trophy – a jack mounted on a wooden base, with an inscription I would not like to repeat here. Even at that point, Jim still wasn't sure whether it was all for real or not until we all burst out laughing, and a smile of realisation crept across his face!

Mal Hughes, the England team manager, with David Icke

The tape of that interview has now been shown at bowls dinners all over Scotland, and Jim will always be remembered as the marker who picked up the jack.

Since then, Jim Barclay has become a great friend and his attitude typifies the good humour you find on the bowls circuit. The players are great characters too, and I only wish we could see more of their humour on the rink. It would, I think, help to build up the game's popularity with the television audiences.

I never cease to be amazed at the skill involved in the game. When I first set foot on an indoor rink and looked down at the jack, a mere dot in the distance, I could not believe how the players could get so close so often. My admiration was confirmed when I had a go myself with Mal Hughes, a top bowler and BBC commentator.

It was on the rink at Preston once again, during an interval at the UK Championship. There are many people who think sports presenters must be good at the sport they are introducing. I can, exclusively, reveal that we are not or, at least, not most of the time anyway. I used to be a professional footballer, but when it comes to bowls, forget it!

When Mal handed me the bowl, it felt pretty heavy and it did look a long way to that jack. I decided that a bit of muscle was called for. The bowl left my hand like a missile, though not of the guided variety. In the blink of an eye it smashed into the ditch at the far end, before launching itself off the rink.

'I think I was a bit strong there, Mal?' 'You could be right,' he said.

Bowls is a bit like golf when you start. You have to understand that it's not in the power as much as the technique. Obviously, I had not appreciated that fact.

I don't know what I had against that far ditch. It had never done anything to me, but I proceeded to launch three more bowls into its care, while the audience watched in astonishment at this idiot trying to wreck the rink. I always did have a touch like an elephant, and I don't think I'll put Bryant under pressure quite yet!

I remember standing on Preston Station the following morning waiting for my train home, when a man came up to me with a smile from ear to ear.

'I say David,' he began, 'I saw you on't bowls yesterday.' 'Good,' I said. 'Did you enjoy it?' 'Aye,' he replied, 'I haven't had such a good laugh for ages – you made yourself look a reet prat!'

With that, I felt it was best to retire gracefully.

I do get great enjoyment from watching others, especially the closing stages of the big games, which always pull out the best from the best. When you see them thread their way through a crowded head to the jack, it can be wonderful television.

But, while I feel that television is a good shop window for the game, the heart and soul of bowls is in the thousands of individual clubs all over the country. Bowls is very big on the Isle of Wight where I live, and it is a pleasure to visit the local clubs because of the atmosphere and friendship they generate. This is what the game of bowls is really about – the television tournaments are only a small part of the sport. Taking part in the game will always be far more important than watching, and that is why bowls will always survive and flourish, whatever happens to its television coverage in the future.

I have immensely enjoyed my time presenting bowls and one thing's for sure: when you are at one of the major tournaments –

with the characters we have on the circuit, your next laugh will never be long in coming. I said at the end of my first bowls tournament, many years ago now, that I found bowls to be a lovely game played by lovely people. I am delighted to say, that this is still true.

Presenting outside broadcasts is very different from working in the main studio. All the technical teams, the directors and the producers like Keith Phillips sit in a big articulated lorry parked outside the venue. It helps to be slim because there isn't much room. The vehicle is called a scanner and carries all the equipment that controls the cameras and the pictures on the screen.

I work, in a makeshift studio, in a room inside the building. I have also broadcast from a dressing room, a chair store, and numerous little side rooms. When I first presented the bowls at the Preston Guild Hall, it was from a room with only three walls! On the other side was a corridor which people had to pass along to get to the bar. Every time they came to me to introduce the next item, someone had to ask passers-by to wait until I'd finished speaking!

During a programme, all the technical and editorial people are sitting in the back of the lorry, while I sit upstairs in the chair store. My goodness, this television lark is glamorous, eh? They talk to me and tell me what's happening through a sort of hearing aid which links me with them. I'm told which piece of action we are going to see next, or whether we are going to live play or a recording, and it is my job to respond to that with the words. Apart from the producer, the most important person, from my point of view, is the production assistant. She controls the timing of the programme and 'runs' the videotape. When you are given a timing for the programme, they don't mean thereabouts, they mean that's how long you have to the precise *second*.

The production assistant (or PA) will count to the end of the transmission: 'Counting out of programme ... ten ... nine ... eight ...' and so on and I have to finish what I have to say at the moment she says zero. There is a department at Television Centre in London called 'presentation', which decides how long each programme will run and whether, in special circumstances, you can have more time at short notice. You should hear some of the animated negotiations that go on in the final minutes of a programme when a match is coming to an end and a few more minutes or seconds are needed to show the finish.

It is sometimes impossible for the programme to be extended, and that is when we have to leave at crucial times in the match. It's not our fault, honest!

Running the videotape, or 'run VT' as it is known in television, is another of the PA's jobs. When we show recorded play, the videotape has to be running for ten seconds before it can be transmitted. If this didn't happen, the picture would be of poor quality. You only get good pictures when the tape is 'up to speed' and that takes approximately ten seconds. This means that the tape has to be run ten seconds before my introduction to each item has finished. So when the PA knows that I have ten more seconds of words to say, she will say 'run VT' and someone in another big articulated lorry will press the button of the videotape machine. The PA then counts out 'ten... nine ... eight' etc., so that I know when my words have to finish.

The question remains – how does the production assistant know when I have ten seconds worth words left to say? Answer: the cue word. We don't have scripts, as such, on outside broadcasts. We make up the programme as we go along, because there is often no other way of doing it. When we are getting close to another 'link' from one videotape to another, maybe from the first set to the third or whatever, I give the PA a word or words. It can be anything from 'Bryant' to 'third set' to 'tough match'. When I say the prearranged cue word or words in my link, the PA says 'run VT' and off we go into the next item. If there isn't time to pass on the cue word, the last resort is to scratch my nose. So, if you ever see me scratch my nose, count from ten and I bet you the pictures will appear on 'zero'.

This method works perfectly well the vast majority of the time, but there can be problems. I remember when I once gave the PA the cue words of 'Cliff Thorburn' at a snooker event, and then realised that I had planned to mention his name *twice* in my link, and that it was the *second* time that I had intended to be the cue. The PA didn't know this, of course, and so she ran the videotape on the first mention. With this, an introduction which I had intended to last 30 or 40 seconds, was cut to about 12 and yours truly had to produce a very hasty change of words to fit.

A SPONSOR'S VIEW

Peter Dyke

Because of the cross-sectional appeal of bowls, the game has sponsors lining up to get involved. The gentlemanly way in which it is played, and the sportsmanlike conduct of the competitors both on and off the green or rink also attracts sponsorship interest. If television continues to broadcast the sport, there will always be national company sponsors to take up either new or existing tournaments on the screen.

Peter Dyke and his wife Sheila congratulating Terry Sullivan on winning the 1985 World Singles Championship at Coatbridge

You only have to consider that magnificent UK Indoor Final in 1989 between David Bryant and David Corkill, the second round match between Margaret Johnson and Tony Allcock, or Brian Duncan winning the Waterloo for the fourth time making history in the 82-year-old handicap, to realise that what was once thought of as a 'geriatric' pastime is now a sport which is filled with excitement and drama.

One of the biggest appeals to a sponsor of bowls is the fact that the game is played in clubs with all the traditional values of sportsmanship. Most clubs have at least a thousand members, which means that the clubs themselves are sponsored. Therefore, when competitions are sponsored, 120,000 competitors are involved in any one tournament, which is especially attractive to a sponsor.

I was the Special Events Executive for Imperial Tobacco Limited for many years, and I remember well how the company first got involved with club sponsorship for an important major bowls championship.

Was it possible to stage an authentic World Indoor Bowls Championship at a small bowling club in Scotland? Monklands District Council, Imperial Tobacco Limited and the national governing bodies certainly thought so. Contracts were signed and, only a few months later, in January 1979, Errol Bungey, a 50-year-old Australian, found himself experiencing snow (some nine inches of it) and sub-zero temperatures for the first time in his life, as he arrived in Glasgow to compete in the first Embassy World Indoor Bowls Championship. This baptism was not exclusive to Errol. His fellow competitors from countries like New Zealand, Canada, Hong Kong and America were similarly taken aback.

This new championship originated from an invitation by Monklands District Council to Imperial Tobacco to sponsor a new national championship in Scotland. They had seen the early success of Embassy's sponsorship of snooker and saw the potential offered by bowls. I discussed this with my board of directors and as a result of that meeting, Monklands was asked if it would be feasible to develop the idea into a World Championship. Any lingering doubts were dispelled on our arrival at the friendly Coatbridge Indoor Bowling Club, just 12 miles east of the city centre where the Championship was to be held for the next nine years. We all knew that the ingredients were right for this major new event.

At this stage of the game's development, players were competing for the glory alone. It was not until 1981 that prize money was acceptable in the game. The total in the first year was £6,250 and the winner, David Bryant, took £2,500. By comparison, 1989 saw 22-year-old Richard Corsie win the Championship and collect £18,000 from a total of £75,000. None of this, in my opinion, has changed the players in any way. It was, and remains, one of the few sports where togetherness and playing the game take precedence over individual egos.

Back to the beginning. How many spectators should we expect? What was the best way to house a sizeable audience in a venue with six rinks and narrow perimeter walkways? The only answer was to put tiered seating on the rinks not in use and to make the necessary alterations to the interior in order to accommodate the BBC television cameras, commentator boxes, the necessary powerful lighting rigs and, for the first time, a remote-controlled overhead camera fixed to the ceiling. This was nicknamed '*hector*', short for High Electronic Camera Travelling Over Rink! At this stage, the BBC were uncertain how many viewers they would attract and, rather cautiously, they restricted their coverage to three half-hour programmes which were transmitted a few days after the event finished. It was a fairly conservative decision taking its cue from the national newspapers which were not given to writing much, if anything, about bowls. Happily times have changed.

To the Coatbridge Directors and Committee it looked as if their once pristine club was under attack, never to be the same again. Was it all going to be worth it? I remember one contractor who, faced with obstruction to his task, decided to use an electric saw to remove one of several three inch thick steel end marker supports. At the time, the Club officials were still in a meeting, discussing the necessity of allowing this seemingly unnecessary destruction. The contractor's excuse was that 'somebody had told him get on with it.' To add fuel to the fire, the sacred Committee Room was converted to accommodate the Press room, the tournament office, hospitality and just about everything else. As a result, the Committee set themselves up in a portakabin outside in the car park, alongside another one which served as a changing room for the players.

When I look back, it is no wonder the club was apprehensive. By the second year, everyone understood and was fully committed to the annual invasion which had certainly put Coatbridge well and truly on the world map. However, for the 1985 Championship, the MDC had pulled out all the stops and somehow found the money to build a splendid extension which meant everyone was now housed inside the club, with their own facilities, plus a bigger restaurant and a special room for a television studio.

By this time, the newly formed World Indoor Bowls Council were co-ordinating the tournament and many of the officials who were originally involved through their own national councils became part of this new body. BBC television coverage had, by now, increased to some 17 hours over seven days. Indoor bowls was well and truly established with millions of viewers.

Undoubtedly, a contributing factor to this popularity was the move from the round robin format and, perhaps more importantly, the many new young players competing and winning at the top level.

1989 saw the combining of the Pairs and Singles into one event which ran for ten days and received nearly 30 hours' television coverage. For the finals, over 1,200 people watched in the comfortable surroundings of the Guild Hall at Preston, whilst a further nine million watched on BBC television, as 22-year-old Richard Corsie won the singles, with veteran David Bryant, teamed with England's number one, Tony Allcock, taking the pairs. All of which, I feel, nicely illustrates the balance which the game has achieved over the years. Surely it can't be long before the ladies also qualify to compete on equal terms?

Whilst a prime objective for any sponsoring company must be to maximise the commercial opportunities that a sport or activity affords them, it is also extremely satisfying and rewarding to be part of a team which continues to bring so much pleasure and enjoyment to an ever increasing audience.

The 1984 World Singles Championship at Coatbridge, with Nigel Smith bowling

A Short History of the Crown Green Game

Keith Phillips

The essential difference between flat and crown green bowling is the surface on which the game is played. Crown greens are undulating, with bumps known as crowns. Some greens have just one crown, others may have two or three, and they can be up to 14 inches high from edge to centre. On the other hand, flat greens, known as rinks, are as level as possible and a standard size of 16 feet wide by 120 feet long.

The methods and techniques of both codes are very different. Crown green bowlers have to concentrate so much on beating the green that they do not indulge much in tactics and strategy, but aim to get as close to the jack as possible. Flat green bowlers, on the other hand, have a much easier task in simply getting close to the jack. Therefore flat green players have to concentrate upon tactics to prevent an opponent from scoring.

It is hard to say when crown green bowling became properly organised. Blackpool Sweepstakes started in 1878, and in 1897 Lancashire and Cheshire combined for the first time to play Warwickshire and Worcester in a series of games. In 1903 the British Crown Green Amateur Association was formed.

In its early days, the sport suffered something of a drawback. The Lord's Day Observance Society wanted to keep Sunday free from sport of any kind, and as the two sides prepared to do battle, the bowlers found that the Church, the Law and the Establishment were lined up on the side of the Observance Society.

However, in 1962, Threlfalls Breweries, now Whitbreads, opened their bowling greens in Manchester, Salford and Liverpool on a Sunday for the first time . Floodlit bowling was in the offing; outdoor winter bowling was just beginning to be popular; handicap bowling was starting to flourish and television was to bring the game to a wider public. Most of the top crown players were, at the time, antagonistic towards any types of game except singles, but television – and money – changed all that.

A very important figure in the development of crown green bowls is undoubtedly Eddie Elson, the retired Secretary of the British Crown Green Bowling Association. He sees his greatest achievement in his time in the 'hot seat' as his success in persuading the BCGBAA to go 'open', hence dropping the word 'amateur' from its title. This enabled the game to attract sponsorship with prize money. Eddie Elson also helped consolidate a single set of crown green rules. He did this in 1980, with the help of Jack Uttley and Jack Isherwood.

LAWS OF THE GAME

There are 41 wide-ranging laws, which cover all aspects of the game. As in all sports there are times when an odd incident occurs which is not specifically anticipated by a particular law, for instance if a strong wind blows a jack off the green. However, to cover every possibility would require a whole volume of rules. The following basic laws are framed to cover singles and pairs; other combinations are seldom played.

1 The leader shall bowl the jack to set a mark which, if it rests on the green must be a distance of not less than 24 yards.

2 The opponent may make an objection after the first bowl has been played, a measurement then takes place to settle the objection.

3 The method of scoring is one point for each bowl nearer to the jack than an opponent's.

4 No player is allowed to change the jack or bowls unless they are damaged so as to be unplayable.

5 If a jack or a bowl is impeded in its course in any way, it is returned to be replayed, but if a player impedes a running bowl both his bowls are forfeited at that end.

6 At the conclusion of an end, neither the jack or any bowl which is claimed to count is allowed to be moved without the consent of the opponent.

7 If a player about the deliver a bowl inadvertently drops it and cannot recover it without quitting the footer, the bowl is considered dead and is taken out of play.

One of the most controversial aspects of the game prior to 1980 was the condonement of the practice of 'stamping' the foot alongside a bowl to endeavour to gain a few more yards. This was never allowed under BCG Rules, but was widespread in many competitions, particularly in the North West. It is now completely outlawed and, after one warning and the loss of a bowl, the offender may have his bowls taken off the green and the game awarded to his opponent.

Here are some of the most important differences between the two codes from the crown green players' angle, plus one or two thoughts that puzzle crown enthusiasts.

Obviously crown greens all vary, because of the undulations and gullies. It is, therefore, possible to place the jack in certain parts of the green and not bowl a wood less than a yard away from the jack. In both codes, the jack is very important because the scoring revolves around which bowls are nearest to it. In crown green, should both bowls from the same player be nearest, they both count as one point each.

If only one is nearest, it is one point only, the same applying in flat green using four bowls (just double up). But there is a considerable difference in the use of the jack. Flat green players use a composition ball similar to a cue ball in snooker. A mark is set by merely rolling it down the rink and, if so requested by the players, the jack can be handled by the official and moved from its original resting place.

Crown green people find this mystifying, for the jack in crown green bowling is an extremely important piece of equipment, governing the whole pattern of the game. It is a smaller replica of the bowls, weighing about 23 oz. Like the bowls, it is eccentric in shape, and biased. The jack is used to determine the length (which could be anything from 19 to 75 yards in any direction), the speed of the green, the bias or peg and the weight or pace. Once it has been led out, it must not be disturbed at all unless it is interfering with another end or is causing some other infringement covered by British Crown Green rules.

There are some really good jack handlers in the crown green game, and their correct manipulation of the 'chitty', 'monkey', 'block', 'little 'un' (some of the nicknames of the jack) has made the difference between winning or losing.

Major BBC TV Crown Green Tournaments

Keith Phillips

The Waterloo

Since 1986 there have been little changes in the organisation, rules and running of the event. What has changed is the way in which the bowlers approach the competition. In its original conception, from when the first bowler trod the sacred turf on the Waterloo bowling green in 1907, this was the tournament in which to earn the money. Although this is still the case to a certain degree (there are now sponsored television tournaments that have larger winning prizes, but not overall prize money), the prestige of winning the Waterloo is still the ultimate of a crown green bowler's career.

In 1907, when Jas Rothwell beat local favourite T. Richardson in the final to win first prize out of a total prize money of £25, there were only 320 entries. In the last few years there were 2,048 entries, the maximum the competition can take. The total prize money was £20,000 with the winner receiving £2,000.

In recent years, the game has expanded tremendously. The bowlers have such an immense choice of tournaments to enter, each with good money prizes, that some of them play in three competitions a day. This influx of prize money has enabled some bowlers to make a living out of the game and their approach to playing has, therefore, changed considerably.

In the old days, they came

Harry Rigby, BBC Bowls commentator

79

straight from work, many just up from the mines, and on to the green to play their matches. They would then go home for a meal. Their equipment consisted of a set of bowls in their overcoat pockets or, for the lucky ones, in their 'dorothy' bags (a bag made from a sleeve of an old overcoat, supposedly invented by a bowler's wife called Dorothy), and that was it.

Today the bowlers are kitted out with T-shirts, sweaters, flannels, shoes, waterproofs, watershoes with overshoes and a change of clothing – all of which they have to carry from event to event. The bowls are carried in expensive leather bowls bags. Nowadays the calendar is so full of competitions that there is no time for re-scheduling matches and players have to be prepared to play in any weather.

The rules of the Waterloo tournament have stood up to the passage of time, the only change coming when Jack Leigh took over in 1981. Up to then bowlers could opt for a 'straw measure', but it was never totally accurate, so Jack banned it from the Waterloo and measures are now carried out by the 'string and tape' measure devices.

The facilities of the Waterloo are second to none in the crown green game, and in the last three years £20,000 has been spent to improve safety due to government legislation. However, before the gates could be opened in 1989, a further £30,000 had to be invested because of the even stricter safety precautions which were considered to be necessary after the terrible Hillsborough soccer stadium disaster. All the money that had to be spent on safety had originally been allocated for improving seating accommodation. Greenall Whitley are hoping that they will soon be able to complete their plan to make the Waterloo even more luxurious than it is now.

Before I write about the 1987, 1988 and 1989 championships, a word about the famous turf. Unlike most greens, bowling ceases completely at the end of September, so that Jack Leigh and his merry bunch can begin maintenance of the green for next season. Through the season, 30,000 pairs of feet have tramped on the grass. It has to be decided whether the green needs 'holetining' or just 'tining'. This means either putting spike holes in the green (tining) or taking a core four inches deep and half an inch in diameter out of the green every three or four inches and throwing them away. This can take three or four tons of soil off the green. The soil is replaced with new soil which has been sterilised and specially treated with chemicals and is, therefore, airy and ready for the new grass to come through. It may surprise many people that there is never any new seed put into the green; it is just left over the winter until mowing begins in the spring.

The number of people playing on the green contributes towards the shifting of the 'crowns' through the season, which is why top bowlers practise on every piece of the green before an important match.

In 1987, the question on everyone's lips was whether Brian Duncan would carry on from the previous when he beat J. Sykes of Mirfield in the final to win two consecutive tournaments, equalling Bernard Kelly's record. He started off determined that he would achieve this goal and, after some difficult matches, got through to the quarter final to meet his chief rival, Noel Burrows from Manchester.

This match will go down in the history of the handicap as one of the best and most exciting ever played on this famous green. Everyone involved said it should have been the final. The game swung from end to end all the way through. Eventually Brian won by the closest of margins, 21–20. The crowd had been on the edges of their seats, watching Brian Duncan further his attempt to beat the record.

In the final he met one of the rising stars of crown green bowling, Robert Eaton. The Waterloo consistently brings through a new name to the top echelons of the sport, and it certainly didn't let anyone down this year. Robert got through to the final with some brilliant bowling and the young 23-year-old won the hearts of the capacity crowd. Unfortunately he met with a ruthless Brian Duncan, who comfortably beat him to win the trophy and equal the record of two consecutive wins.

The 1988 Waterloo Handicap was unique in the fact that it threw up three possibilities for a place in the history of the event. First of all, could the number one crown green star, Brian Duncan, break his own existing record (held equally with Bernard Kelly of Hyde) and become the first man to win the event in three consecutive years?

Secondly, could he break the record held by Kelly for the

highest number of consecutive round wins. Kelly won in 1953 and 1954 and was beaten in the fourth round in 1955. This meant his consecutive wins amounted to 23 – 10 in 1953, 10 in 1954 and three in 1955. The entry in those days was 1024. Brian Duncan had 22 consecutive wins behind him, 11 each in 1987 and 1988 because, with the number of entries now at 2,048, an extra round is played. Thirdly, could Duncan be the first bowler to win the spring and summer handicaps in the same year?

None of it was to be. Duncan met up with David Greatwich of Ashton-under-Lyne in the first round and was beaten 15–21. So all the records are still intact.

The fact that Duncan went out in the first round, beaten by a 'nobody', illustrates that the 'minnows' in the game can alter the pages of history. This is, of course, largely due to the fact that there are no seeds. Apart from previous winners who are handicapped two shots for every year they win, all the players start on the same footing. This lasts for five years.

Young players are, without doubt, coming through to challenge the established bowling stars, but in 1988 it was the turn of the veterans to prove that bowls can be played at any age. Ingham Gregory, a professional bowler throughout his career, and well-known in the panel game, began to fight his way through to the finals. He was almost unnoticed, until he defeated Alan Broadhurst, one of the new young favourites after the demise of Brian Duncan in the semi-final. The book-makers made Broadhurst the odds-on favourite for the match, but to everyone's astonishment Ingham Gregory defeated him.

In the finals he faced Glynn Cookson, who had been beaten in the semi-final in 1987 by Robert Eaton. Cookson took a commanding lead of 17–5. Despite a minor comeback by Eaton, Ingham Gregory took the title and achieved his greatest ambition at the age of 64. Sadly he passed away the following spring, after a long illness, so was not able to defend his title.

In 1989, the 'King of the Waterloo', Brian Duncan, won the handicap for the fourth time, thus setting another record. 'Handicap' was a key word for this remarkable man's game. From the first round onwards he had to give every bowler that he played four shots. As he ploughed through the field, using his formula of playing the corners, his form was devastating.

The final was against Kevin Wainwright from Warrington, an outsider at the start of the competition, who started off five with Duncan off one. The five handicap is for all bowlers in the Waterloo. It is designed to allow more games to be played and, therefore, to give more bowlers the opportunity to gain entry to the competition. Duncan's handicap of one was due to his previous wins during the last five years.

Wainwright took one at the first end to make it 1–6 after laying two down. Duncan won ends two and three 4–6. Wainwright managed to pick up another at the fourth and the fifth to make it 4–8. Duncan bounced back at the sixth with a double, 6–8. It had all the makings of a close final until Duncan levelled at the eleventh to make the score 10–10. He didn't look back, going on to win handsomely at 21–12.

Duncan intends to carry on winning top competitions because of the thrill of the big time occasion. He says, 'The time you don't get a thrill is the time you start losing.' His opponent, Keven Wainwright, admitted to tears that day at home. He

Jack Leigh with the late Ingham Gregory at the 1988 Waterloo

asked himself, 'Why am I crying?' He then realised the significance of the occasion – to be in the final of the Waterloo, and to be in the final day's play, is something in itself. To be in the final and play the 'King' is a tremendous bonus, and to have been the winner would have fulfilled his ambition.

On a final note, another landmark in the history of the Waterloo will be made next year when Brian Duncan starts off the tournament playing off 'scratch'.

Top Crown 1987

On 4 June, a large contingent of BBC outside broadcast vehicles left Manchester to travel to the Isle of Man. It was to be the first time a bowls competition of any note was televised from the island. To make the trip economical, the team also recorded two other programmes following the *Top Crown* event.

The players, officials and all the BBC staff were looking forward to a pleasant weekend's work in the sun at the beginning of June, but fate was not on our side. The Friday, which was our rig day and also the 500 cc TT motorcycle championship day, heralded the rain, which poured down on the Saturday and Sunday of the recording, and meant that the cameramen had to constantly wipe their camera lenses for two days. It was so wet that I could only use three out of the five cameras covering the bowling at any one time, because the other two had to be wiped in rotation.

The rain also depleted the numbers of spectators. I suspect that if the weather had been its usual warm and sunny mixture at the beginning of June, we would have had a full house. Unfortunately, the female players were at a distinct disadvantage in the wet conditions, and didn't make the second round.

The top half of the draw had the two pairs most fancied to take the trophy – Roy Armson and Noel Burrows and Tommy Johnstone and Eddie Hulbert. The lower half was much more open after the demise of the holders Duncan and Fletcher, who went out in the first round to the Cumbrian pair, Nevinson and Edmonson. They, in turn, were beaten in the second round by that popular pair from Cheshire, Stan Frith and Brian Prolze. Frank Kitchen and Mike Eccles from Merseyside had a good result in beating Mel Evans and John Turner from Cannock in the Midlands, a fancied pair who have won 13 pairs titles since 1979. This was a popular win as Frank Kitchen had worked so hard to get to a top television tournament in the Isle of Man.

As predicted, Burrows and Armson and Johnstone and Hulbert reached the semi-finals, with Noel and Roy eventually coming out at 21–16. Frank and Mike also reached the semi-finals, but they were ousted by Gerald Gregson and Alan Shacklady.

British grand prix racing driver, Nigel Mansell, who presented the trophy, watched the final in reasonably good weather. He must know somebody influential in the weather world! The outcome was as expected, with the 1987 Pairs champions, Armson and Burrows, winning a comfortable 21–10.

Frank Kitchen didn't quite lose out on everything. He played all his matches in the pouring rain, but Frank wore a stylish tartan weatherproof outfit. It was to become the envy of players, spectators and viewers alike. When the programme was eventually transmitted, he had a large number of letters from viewers asking where they could buy one of his tartan outfits.

TOP CROWN 1988

1988 saw the last of the BBC2 Top Crown Pairs competitions. It was played at the very picturesque Mitchell and Butlers Sports Ground at Portman Road in Birmingham. Once again the ladies were present, but again they only managed to set one pair to the second round – Pat Davies and Karen Galvin. They were beaten by Andrew Spragg and David Platts from Derbyshire. This young pair were well supported by the Midlands spectators and they reached the semi-final stages with some excellent bowling.

The holders, Armson and Burrows, favourites to be the first pair to retain the title, were, unfortunately, knocked out in the quarter-finals by the finalists Peter Varney and Bob Gilfillan. The other fancied pairing, Duncan and Fletcher, were slaughtered in the semi-finals 21–8 by Ken Strutt and Tommy Heyes, a well-known pair on the crown green circuit.

The final turned out to be a classic cliff-hanger. Tit for tat, the lead changed constantly, with never more than two or three shots in it. In the end Ken and Tommy took the trophy and the £2,000 prize money, winning a cracking match at 21–20.

MORE STARS OF THE CROWN GREEN GAME

Keith Phillips

VERNON LEE

Vernon is better known to television viewers as the 'dancing master'. He puts on a lively act for the crowd, crossing over the woods whilst they are in progress across the green and giving some energetic entertainment for the spectators wherever he plays. He became a panel professional around 1960 and competed for 17 years alongside many famous players of the past – Tom Mayor, the 1963 Waterloo winner; Seth Wane; Tedbar Tinker, the 1944 Waterloo winner; Neil Norris; Jack Taylor and Ingham Gregory, the 1988 Waterloo champion who died shortly after his win. They are all now deceased, but are well remembered by Vernon. Famous names of today, like Brian Duncan and Roy Armson, were also panel men around the same time as Lee.

Vernon Lee was born in Shaw near Oldham in 1925 and started bowling at the age of 11. He played on Westwood Park, Oldham, and then went on to Chadderton Cot Bowling Club and recalls the great players of those days like Tich Whitehead, Jimmy Wilson, Jimmy Brown and Austin Lever, the short round peg expert from Clarksfield.

In the 1950s and 1960s, there weren't as big handicaps around like there are today. Lee won the Crown Hotel championship at Stockport in the late 1950s, out of 1,024 runners, beating Maurice Courtney of Blackley in the final.

However, Vernon's greatest ambition was to win the Waterloo and in 1980 he beat Frank Kitchen in the semi-final. Frank was a former rugby league international and is now the top organiser for ITV's bowls coverage. In the final, Lee then came up against another Vernon, Glyn Vernon from Winsford Liberal Club in Cheshire. It is a final that is remembered as one of the best ever played at the Waterloo. BBC commentator Harry Rigby regards it as the best final he has seen since the 1950s.

Vernon Lee, the 'dancing master' of crown green, in mid-flight

Vernon Lee beat Glyn Vernon 21–20, after a match that saw Glyn Vernon stand for the match and title three times in the closing stages. But Lee refused to bow out. He snatched a dramatic victory after dancing all over the green, into the hearts of the crowd and into the pages of the bowls history books. He also picked up the title of crown green bowling's 'dancing master'.

87

When asked whether the changes in the rules and the attitudes of the referees affected him, he claimed that it did. He had been warned many times to keep away from the woods (as per the rule book), but claims that he only did it to entertain the crowd and not to gain any advantage. He felt that the BBC were also keen for him to do it. Also, he has always been very energetic in his approach to sporting activities!

He feels that the people who run the game are a little to blame because they try to organise it like a Sunday school outing. Because the bowlers are playing for big money, he thinks that the game is bound to attract people with character and flair. He feels that players may be a little over-restricted by zealous officials and, therefore, will not be as entertaining for the crowds.

People always turned out when Vernon Lee's name was on the card. He became Crown King in 1985 and picked up the Tetley Walker and the North Lancs Fylde Merit in the same year.

Vernon feels that bowls is no longer an 'old man's game' and that there are some very good young players around. Despite a family tragedy that left his son Bryan paralysed and took the edge off his own game for some time, the 'dancing master' of the crown greens has a good few more steps left before approaching anything like the last waltz. Vernon will always be remembered as one of the game's greatest characters – dance on Vernon.

John 'Banjo' Bancroft

This 25-year-old bowler from Hyde in Cheshire plays with James North's bowling club and, over the last decade, has come through the ranks to emerge as one of the most attractive players in the crown green game. He started playing bowls at the age of 11 at the Talbot Hotel in Hyde, and then moved to the Denton Cricket and Bowling Club. It was there that he picked up his 'banjo' nickname, given to him by his lively young bowling colleagues, some of whom are still playing with him in the big time handicaps and in county sides.

John won the big Manchester Evening News Handicap in 1986 and then picked up the ITV Bass Masters title in 1988. He has played Brian Duncan eight times, winning five games. In 1989 he won the famous Talbot Handicap at Blackpool, and he has high hopes of winning the Waterloo in the future. A victory there would put him alongside Duncan as one of the few men to have done the double.

John's style has made him a big favourite with the crowds wherever he plays and on form he is one of the hardest men to beat. He is also a very good flat green player, but feels he has quite a bit to prove yet at the crown green game.

One of the things that has motivated John is the 'Italian connection'. His wife Gill is the daughter of Tony Trezza (Bella Bella). The attractive Gill follows John around the circuit and poppa Tony, who plays with the same club in Hyde, is a considerate critic about 'Banjo's' progress in the top circuit. He still thinks he can teach John a thing or two about bowls. On more than one occasion, John has been glad to hear a cry of 'Putta a yarda inna the nexta bowla' from his father-in-law, who is a very popular figure in the Tameside area. John's father Neville and his mother Val are also excellent players and are a good double act on the greens.

John would like to see the return of singles on BBC television and, of course, to win a BBC event himself. He is a member of the Greater Manchester County team and would dearly love to win the British Crown Green County title with them. It is well within the realms of possibility that his father-in-law, who came to the UK around 30 years ago, could be on the same county

John 'Banjo' Bancroft

team as John, and a good many judges can vouch for his ability at county level.

John Bancroft has matured into a player of the highest class and, given an average break or two, the future must hold many more successes for this crown green champion player.

MICHAEL LEACH

Michael, who was born in St Annes in 1947, plays for the Newton Hall Club in Blackpool and the Hope Street Recreation in St Annes. He reached a great peak in his bowling career when he won the British Crown title at Cleckheaton in Yorkshire (what a cheek, a Lancashire man winning a British title in Yorkshire!). It was gained at the expense of another Lancastrian, Vernon Seddon from Widnes.

When he first started playing, Michael had a very unorthodox manner of sending out his woods. Once, when on his way to the BBC Top Crown Doubles title in partnership with Noel Burrows, his delivery was described by BBC commentator Harry Rigby as 'worse than that of a one-armed midwife'. Then, with just one or two 'mods' he went on to pick up several big events.

Following his 1984 title year, he developed a form of 'dartitis' and was out of the game for three years. However, he is now back on the 'mat' and is playing well again. In 1989 Michael reached the final of the Pairs at Worthing in the English Championships – his partner was another great north country character, Charlie Tattersall of Blackpool. He speaks highly of the organisation at Worthing and the wonderful treatment that both he and his partner 'Charlie Tatt' were given. He also looks forward to going back annually, with a view to doing a bit more winning of course.

Michael has worked in the BBC commentary box as a summariser and made his debut as a commentator on the Ladies' final at the 1989 Waterloo. He has a great future in television, as he is not afraid to speak his mind. Although he is a devotee of crown green bowling, he speaks very highly of flat green and is now finding himself getting more involved at top level.

Michael has some definite views about various aspects of bowling – in both codes – and feels that the crown green referees could do with a lesson or two from their flat green counterparts.

He thinks that, at times, the crown men are a bit over zealous in applying their authority and would welcome a less rigid approach. He would also be in favour of introducing the use of wedges in crown green measures under bowls during the taping of tilted woods. The standard of dress for crown green players is also something that he feels could be improved upon.

With regard to his form, Michael thinks that he is back to a very high standard, but not quite to what he was in the early 1980s. To give an example of how much he has progressed since his 'hiccups' phase, on the day following the 1989 Waterloo final (when Brian Duncan won his record fourth title) Michael came out of the 'commentary' box to play in the McKinley event. It contained all the champions (Duncan included). Michael reached the final, losing to another great young champion, Martin Gilpin from Cumbria, 31–25.

Jeremy Muff

Nobody could really imagine that a Yorkshire Midland-based general manager for Ansell's Brewery, who gained an honours degree in classics at Queens College Oxford, would go on to become one of crown green's top performers.

Jeremy was born in Brighouse in 1958 and started bowling at the age of 13. He had to leave the game between 1977 and 1981 to pursue his studies at Oxford, but returned to the bowling scene in 1982 and won the Yorkshire Parks Individual Merit in his first full year's bowling for four years. In 1983 he picked up a major title – the Wilson's Brewery Open at the Church Inn in Rochdale, plus £1,000. His employers could not have minded him taking money from one of their brewery competitors. Jeremy was in the Yorkshire County Parks Championship team of 1982 and moved into the Yorkshire crown green camp in 1983, winning the county home team average prize in his first full season in the Yorkshire county crown green ranks.

Jeremy 'emigrated' to Sandbach in Cheshire in 1988, but that did not interfere with his loyalty to Yorkshire. He picked up the Tetley/Walker title at Warrington, which qualified him for his television debut. He also went on to win a very high class '16' at Bunbury Bowling Club in the heart of Cheshire.

Jeremy's opinion of the flat game is that it is not as interesting

Jeremy Muff

as crown green which, he feels, provides more of a challenge because of the variations of the greens and the weather.

One of Jeremy's ambitions is to become the top Yorkshire player. He would also like to join Brian Duncan at the top, although he admits that that would be quite a feat. He has entered the Waterloo every year since 1983 and, like every other player with any sort of ambition, he wants the title, although he still finds the Waterloo green hard to play. In 1989, however, he reached the last 16 and hopes to improve on that in the coming year.

The 1989 Waterloo convinced Jeremy that he would like to see someone appointed to do nothing else but market the game.

ROB EATON

26-year-old Rob Eaton from Holmes Chapel started on the bowling trail at the age of 14 in 1977. Now several years later, he has become quite a well-known figure, particularly at the Waterloo green. He is the son of a mid-Cheshire farming family. His father, Ricky, and mother, Norah, are both very good crown green players, but it's the boyish-looking Rob who has made everyone sit up and watch.

In 1987 he came from the any price section of the outsiders laid by the Blackpool book-makers at the Waterloo. Some of the bets offered included a fortnight's holiday, full-board at a hotel

Rob Eaton at the Waterloo

and £100 a week for life. But this quiet, seemingly unflappable, young man produced some great bowling going on to reach the final and take part in an historic match with Brian Duncan. True, Duncan won 21–11, but Rob had him worried until 11–11. Rob had put himself up amongst the best, coming from milking cows to almost doing the same to the Blackpool book-makers.

Viewers really took to this unassuming young farmer, who went on to prove that 1987 Waterloo was no flash-in-the-pan. He reached the Waterloo quarter-finals the following year, where he lost to Glyn Cookson, another bright young Cheshire star. It proved to everyone how well he played the Waterloo arena. Rob bobbed up again in 1989 and reached the semi-finals, where he lost to Brian Duncan on his way to his record-breaking fourth Waterloo victory.

Rob's club is Good Companions of Holmes Chapel in Cheshire. He is one of the rarities in bowls – a playing official and a club secretary, who also plays in the Knutsford league, winning the league average in 1989. He has made six appearances in the Cheshire county side to date but, no doubt, has quite a few more caps to come in the future. He won the Alan Bratt Memorial at Pochins, Middlewich, beating another top Cheshire county man, Bob Crawshaw, in the final.

Rob is well-respected wherever he plays due to the great sporting attitude he adopts, whether he wins or loses. Although he has been a key figure in Duncan's record round-up of Waterloo victories he has, I believe, his own record of making the final day (ie the last eight out of 2,048 entries) in three consecutive years. He was runner-up to Duncan in 1987; a quarter-finalist in 1988 and semi-finalist in 1989.

Not bad for a young farmer. Rob has cultivated that green acre at the back of the Waterloo as if it were part of his own land. All the indications are that he will be back in the future and that the nation's television audiences will welcome this young man who looks just as much at home at the Waterloo as he does on the homestead at Holmes Chapel.

A final word. One reason that Rob is so good on the turf may be that he picked up a Bachelor of Science degree at Nottingham University in 1983 – on soil science. No wonder he finds it easy to put his bowls on the right land and to miss all the worm casts!

THE LADIES' GAME

Keith Phillips

FLAT GREEN

Ladies' bowls goes back to the 16th century, but it wasn't until the 1900s that it really began to organise itself as a recognised sporting body. The English Womens Bowling Association was formed in 1931 and the rest followed.

Television has brought to light many sports submerged within themselves, but only those whose members have the incentive and the courage to change with the times and to modernise their game have succeeded in being recognised in their own right.

It seems that only a very few lady bowlers are willing to speak out in favour of updates which would enable them to reap some reward for all the travelling and financial outlay they have to endure. This doesn't mean that they don't love the sport, because they obviously do, but modernising the approach would certainly make life a lot easier for the existing younger players who put a lot of themselves into the sport. In saying this, I have talked to many people involved in the game of level green bowls and have come to the following conclusions.

Ladies' bowls on its own is *not* attractive to the general public. Mixed bowls *is*. Men's bowls is *fairly* attractive. So we do need the ladies competing with the men to get the best out of the sport, particularly from the point of view of media and television coverage.

History was made in indoor bowling when Superbowl invited ladies into its non-ranked competition and again, in October 1989, with the UK Indoor championships. Two ladies were invited to play in this ranking tournament on level terms with the men. They were Margaret Johnston, the holder of the World Indoor Singles championship for two years running, and the 1988 UK Indoor champion, Joyce Lindores.

Joyce was knocked out in the first round, but Margaret made it to the second and came up against the number one level green bowler in the world, Tony Allcock. Until the final, his was the match of the championship, and Margaret was considered a little unlucky not to have won. At the crucial moment, with the score at two sets all and 6–6 in the deciding set, she played one of the few weak shots of her game, and Tony pinched the match.

This match has done the ladies' lobby a power of good, as there seems to be only one other lady at the top men's standard – Norma Shaw from Durham. Both these ladies regard playing the men as a challenge which has brought about the beginning of a revolution in major televised championships. The ladies will be invited if the standards are high enough. Criticism was levelled when Margaret Johnston was invited to play because she hadn't won her own club championship. This is the difference between running local club competitions and large televised tournaments. Most of the top men don't necessarily win their club championships, but they have proved their class in front of the cameras, with all the added pressures that that brings.

A good analogy is in snooker, where the stars often get beaten in their local clubs, but a local club player may not be able to withstand the pressures of a major televised championship. The officials of the WIBC admit that they are only now beginning to know the players that can compete under such pressurised situations. How much of this kind of pressure the ladies can take is still an unknown quantity.

How many ladies are there who can produce the standard of bowls played by Margaret Johnston in two major television competitions – the Superbowl and the UK Indoor Championship? The WIBC think that the ladies' involvement is so important that they are making a concerted effort to encourage ladies to try to qualify, isolating more of the stronger players and inviting them into the bigger competitions.

Also high on the list of the WIBC's priorities is to try to get bowlers to relax a bit more and to show their emotions. Their behaviour on the rink is of utmost importance – this applies to both men and ladies. They want them to involve the audience, and to let the viewers see how they feel. To the general public, one of the attractions of television bowls is that the viewer is given magnificent close-ups of players and these would be enhanced by some emotion coming through.

The Victorian codes of practice must be modernised. These are more widely followed in the outdoor game, particularly the ladies' outdoor game where players have been, and still are, taught not to show their opponent the way they feel. It cuts both ways!

One of the problems of bringing the ladies' game into the 20th century is the concern that their traditional organisation will be interfered with. When indoor televised bowls started, the same problem confronted the men. They were given a guarantee that their established customs would not be tampered with and the British Isles Indoor and Outdoor, all non-televised events, national competitions etc. are still played as they always have been.

Another major problem that has been brought up by a number of top class lady bowlers is that of dress. The ladies world uniforms are completely out of date and, as one top men's official put it, the 'silly hats' that they play in should be abolished whilst playing on the rink, together with the drab uniform.

The existing code of dress is partly to blame for the lack of young ladies taking up the sport. Potential younger players must be completely put off when they see these out-of-date uniforms on television.

As rapidly as the sport is growing in the men's world, so it would seem that it is declining in the ladies' game. Many of the participants give the impression that they don't want to expand their horizons or to look outside their traditional rules and regulations. They appear to be happy this way which, of course, is their prerogative. But what a shame that more younger players with the style of Margaret Johnston are not being encouraged into the sport. The bowls public would be delighted if some exciting, young personalities came to the forefront of ladies' bowls.

LADIES' PROFILES

Margaret Johnston

Margaret was born in Upperlands, County Londonderry, Northern Ireland, in 1943 and started her bowling career in 1964, two weeks after her baby was born. Her church minister formed a

Margaret Johnston

short mat club and, together with her husband, she won 27 competitions in one year. Her husband eventually joined the Ballymoney Outdoor Club in 1977 and Margaret followed him in 1979. She entered the Singles of the Irish Championships and was beaten in the final.

In 1981, Margaret was selected for the international team and has been in it ever since. She played outdoor in the summer and short mat in the winter until 1986, when the Ballymoney club built an indoor stadium. Margaret joined and, with her outdoor successes, managed to get into the indoor national team. In the same year, she won the British Isles Indoor Singles title. In 1985, she had won the B.I. Outdoor Singles and Pairs titles and in 1986 won the Pairs gold medal in the Commonwealth Games in Edinburgh with Nan Allely as her partner. Her performances and achievements went from strength to strength. Just look at this record:

1987 World Indoor Singles champion – Llanelly.

1988 World Indoor Singles champion – Edinburgh.

1988 Gold medal, World Outdoor Pairs, with Phillis Nolan.

1988 Superbowl finalist, beaten by David Corkill.

To add to her long list of achievements, Margaret has been picked to play for Ireland in the singles at the New Zealand Commonwealth Games.

Margaret is another bowler who feels that the uniform should be modernised – because the present design is not practical. She advocates culottes rather than skirts and feels that participants should be allowed to remove their hats when they play. The reason given for the wearing of hats is that they stop the ladies' hair being blown out of place. Ladies are also encouraged to not show their emotions because if they smile it might 'crack' their make-up! If this is so, then the rules should certainly be altered. How can a lady concentrate on her bowling if she is worrying about these problems at the same time. Margaret also feels that more encouragement should be given to the younger girls to persuade them to take up the game seriously.

Norma Shaw

Norma was born in 1937 near Wakefield, Yorkshire. She started playing crown green bowls in Wakefield with her husband, but it wasn't until they moved to the North East that they started playing flat green bowls. They joined the local club and played in the local league, where they both won their singles competitions.

1973 was the year that Norma really headed for the higher echelons of the sport. She qualified for the county championships at Wimbledon in both the singles and pairs. She won the singles and, since then, has never looked back. The county championships were moved to Leamington Spa and in 1977/8, Norma was nominated for the Durham county team.

Norma Shaw

The highlight of her career was in 1981 when she was chosen to go to Toronto for the World Championships. She won the gold in the singles and the bronze in the pairs. Although they had been called a 'scratch' team, the team as a whole won the overall trophy and a further two gold medals. Since then Norma has toured Australia twice and New Zealand once, unsuccessfully defending her world singles title in 1985 in Australia against local heroine Merle Richardson. She has been picked, once again, for the Commonwealth Games fours team as number three.

Norma points out that one of the major differences between men and women bowlers is that women will nearly always try to 'draw' themselves out of trouble, while the men will always 'fire'. She thinks that ladies should 'fire', more often. They apparently feel embarrassed if they miss with a firing shot. She should know because she played the great David Bryant in one of the first indoor bowling competitions to be shown on British network television – the John Player Classic held at the indoor rink at Darlington. The competition was shown on *Grandstand* in the 1970s.

Norma feels that the ladies should try to express themselves to the spectators more than they do. She remembers Mary Price appealing and playing to the English supporters in an England v Scotland match, in Scotland. Although there were far less English than Scottish supporters, they eagerly responded to her, which undoubtedly helped the England team make a great comeback when they were way behind.

She would like to see the Ladies' World Singles (Indoors) Championship on television, but thinks that they would only just make the 32 starters by including some players from overseas. Like many other top lady bowlers, Norma also feels, that although she enjoys the way the game is played, the sport should try to modernise its image.

CROWN GREEN

Since the first edition of *The BBC Book of Bowls* was published, the ladies in the crown green game have really flourished. They have now become fully affiliated to the BCGBA and are represented on the full committee. Numerous new clubs have sprouted up and ladies crown green bowling clubs now stretch from Coventry to the northern counties, right up as far as Cumbria.

They are getting more sponsorship from leading companies and in 1989 Yorkshire Bank announced that it was putting up a sum of £1,710. Thomas Taylor donated £2,000 for the Ladies'

Barbara Rawcliffe

Champion of Champions event. The British Parks Merit, as predicted in the first edition, now has 2,000 entries, but the most significant achievement in the outdoor ladies' game is the fact that they had three entrants in the Bass Masters last season. They were 1988 winner, Barbara Rawcliffe; Yorkshire Bank champion Sheila Speed and that most popular lady from the Wirral, Pat Davies.

Perhaps even more of an achievement for the ladies

integrating with the men was that Mary Ashcroft (who founded the Ladies' Waterloo) refereed the Bass Masters Championship. This would have been unheard of a few years ago.

LADIES' WATERLOO 1988

This was the first time a full Ladies' tournament had been televised during the semi-final and final stages. BBC2's Top Crown Pairs competition was the first television tournament to allow ladies to compete on equal terms with the men. This was in 1986 when two ladies' pairs were invited to play. Karen Galvin and Mary Farmer won their way to the semi-finals, where they were beaten by the eventual winners, Brian Duncan and Norman Fletcher. Their performance was so impressive that the BBC decided to record highlights of the Ladies' Waterloo in 1988 to fit into its Waterloo Handicap schedule. This, too, proved to be a good decision and the winner turned out to be Barbara Rawcliffe of Poulton-le-Fylde, who beat Anne O'Loughlin in great style in the final.

A total prize money of £4,500 was at stake, with 1,200 entrants going for the trophy and a first prize of £1,000. Right from the beginning of final's day, Barbara played just to a mark, and with opponents constantly querying the length the measurers seemed to be on the green all the time. But she kept to her strategy and, considering that she only took up bowls in 1978, she went from strength to strength – keeping the large crowd on the edge of their seats in many of her games.

In the quarter-final, against Sylvia Royle from Altrincham, she was involved in yet another closely contested match. Barbara just managed to 'pip Sylvia at the post', going through at 21–20.

In the semi-final she came up against what was, on paper, her toughest match yet, against the previous Ladies' Waterloo champion, Karen Galvin. Karen was one of the ladies who spearheaded them into television exposure in the 1986 Top Crown Pairs, reaching the semi-final stages before going out to Duncan and Fletcher.

Recognised for a long time as the top lady crown green bowler, Karen had difficulty in coping with Barbara's short game in this absorbing semi-final. As Barbara began to go into a positive

102

lead, Karen tried everything to get her game together, querying jack lengths and bowls in the head. She finally succumbed and Barbara took the match 21–15 to go into the final.

Anne O'Loughlin from Birmingham had just beaten Carol Brown from Manchester in her semi-final. She started off the final with a lot of confidence and, with the score at ll–ll, everyone was looking forward to another cliffhanger. But Barbara Rawcliffe wasn't having any of that. Getting the jack, back came her devastating short game and she eventually ran out a comfortable 21–15 winner.

Everybody agreed that televising a ladies' championship was a success.

LADIES' WATERLOO 1989

The second year of television for the Ladies' Waterloo provided viewers with an outstanding final, with Diana Hunt from Warrington winning the title 21–20 over Pat Holt of Great Harwood. It was a dream come true for Diana, who had come through to the final stage from the 1,024 starters in previous years. Her previous best performances were in reaching finals day in 1984 and the last 32 in 1986.

It has to be said that Diana had the easier passage through to the final. Pat Holt bowled out C. Bush from Lytham in the second round. C. Bush had defeated the title holder Barbara

Rawcliffe in the first round. Pat then went on to beat the 1987 winner, Pat Davies from Wirral, in the third round and then had a magnificent win over the 1986 champion, Maureen Bresnan, also from the Wirral. All had looked lost for Pat when she was 16–20 down, but sheer doggedness enabled her to 'claw' her way back five singles in a row, to win 21–20, getting into the final.

Diana Hunt

REFEREES AND UMPIRES
Keith Phillips

UMPIRES AND MARKERS

Flat Green Bowling

Ten years ago, it was decided that umpires and markers should have a training scheme. They were given copies of the laws of the game and were then required to sit a paper, where they were asked questions to see whether they could interpret the laws. After this they were presented with a written and oral examination which they had to pass at 75% before they were accepted. The assumption from this is that every flat green umpire has a wide and full knowledge of all the rules and laws of the game. It then remains to be seen whether the umpire has the commonsense to use the acquired knowledge during a match.

The game is about players, not umpires. When you go to a game the umpire should make his decision and then stay in the background. The best umpire is the one that is barely noticed. If he makes the right decision at the right time, and doesn't cause embarrassment to the spectators, players or to anyone else on the rink or green, that is the man that the official body is looking for.

Things have changed during the ten years of training umpires. Originally the game started with very little professional equipment and with non-professional experts acting as umpires.

Television has revolutionised the approach adopted by umpires. They are now very aware that, during a televised event, they are under close scrutiny from the players, the spectators and, in particular, from the television viewers. The audience watching at home feels they are the best judge because they are all experts and, most being bowlers, think they have a superior knowledge of the game.

Jimmy Barclay holding up 2 'lollipops' to indicate 2 shots

This is a major problem for the senior umpire, Jimmy Barclay, and has led to the production of a professional umpires kit. Due to the circumstances that have evolved, a measuring system has been produced whereby umpires can measure from nil to the longest distance from the jack and on different planes, either in the ditch or on the green.

The one thing that has still not been resolved is the ideal way to measure bowls of close proximity. The sonic measure which was introduced in 1984 will not now be officially used in major televised events, as it is affected by interference of close bowls. Until a measure has been invented to sit between the bowls and which guarantees an exact reading, traditional methods will continue to be used.

It has also been found that the umpire and the marker now have a function other than that which was originally intended, that is interpreting the laws of the game. When crown green bowlers were introduced to the UK Indoor Singles at Preston – the heart of the crown green game – they and the spectators demanded to know who was lying shot by how many, distances etc. This was unheard of in the flat game, so 'lollipops' were introduced to give players and spectators full information as to what was happening on the rink. The colours on the 'lollipop' showed whose bowls were closest to the jack. This system has been responsible for the major change in the duties of the umpires and markers. It is invaluable to players, journalists, television commentators and scorers during major television championships.

A training video for umpires is in the process of being made. It will make bowling umpires even more professional in the future and will, eventually, standardise umpiring methods at all levels, wherever the game is played.

Several questions which have been raised about umpires and indoor rinks are now being studied. The age factor and the fitness of the umpires as well as the problem of the heat generated by the television lights, are amongst them. It is hoped that, in the near future, these points will be resolved, ensuring a near-perfect system of umpiring in the flat game.

Another major problem that still exists in the flat game is that there are tremendous differences in the rules of the game played between the southern and the northern hemispheres of the world. For example, in South Africa, Australia and New Zealand a line is drawn on the green right down the centre, from the jack to the mat. In the UK a few dots, only about a yard long, from the jack down the centre line towards the mat, have just been authorised. The white line down the whole of the centre of the rink obviously aids the placing of the jack and the mat and helps the player who constantly drives – a style of play more readily played in the southern hemisphere.

The flat game has also had to resolve the slowness of matches. This has largely been rectified in the indoor game, particularly in televised events, by placing monitors at each end of the rink so that the players can see the head without walking. However, this only applies to the players' first two bowls each, because once there are four bowls in the head, it is difficult to judge distances without going and actually looking at it close hand. The outdoor game, with its traditions going back much longer in time, will be more difficult to speed up. However, if members want television coverage, it will have to be speeded up. No television company or sponsor wants to televise bowls players going for long walks – it means having to edit and throw miles of tape into the bin which is a waste of time and money.

The younger members of the umpiring fraternity have learnt to think metric, but the majority of umpires, being of the old school, still think in feet and inches. One of the functions of the umpire in flat green bowling is to measure any jack laid that is not 25 yards length.

One particular umpire had a measure that was yards on one side and metres on the other. She then had to measure for a suspect short jack. Not familiar with the conversion from yards to metres, she measured the distance in metres and then instructed the game to go on. Once the match had started, she talked to a colleague, confessing her confusion. The colleague explained that all she had to do was turn the tape over to see the equivalent in yards. Realising then that the jack was short, she stopped the game and had the players re-start. That umpire was very unpopular for quite a while.

The advent of television has also encouraged the umpires' organisation in level green bowling to look at the snooker game.

The referees in snooker have devised objects to put around the balls for cleaning and marking. The bowling umpires are now experimenting with a similar object to put round the jack when a measure takes place. This will greatly reduce the possibility of the jack being accidentally moved.

Finally, there has always been a little friction between the outdoor and indoor organisations, apart from the umpires who officiate in both areas. As the players on the top level are the same ones as those who compete both indoor and outdoor, this may eventually bring the organisations together.

REFEREES

Crown Green Bowling

As with flat green bowling, it was about ten years ago that referees first had to sit an examination before being able to take part in competitions. However, to become a grade 'A' referee, their pass level was 90%. There is no doubt that since the introduction of the examination, the standards of refereeing in crown green has also improved beyond recognition.

Although the umpires in flat look more organised, it must be remembered that in crown green competitions there are sometimes four matches being played at the same time, covering the whole of the green and all going in different directions. This makes it extremely difficult for the referee. The television viewer often doesn't recognise this fact, because they are only shown one match at a time. But, despite the differences in the method of play and the number of bowlers on the green, the same principles apply to crown referees as they do to flat green umpires. They have to be in the right place, make the right decision, and keep everyone involved happy.

One of the differences in rules between the two codes is that in flat green, the bowls are wedged before measures, whilst in crown they are not. Many crown officials believe this should happen in their game as well. But the flat code has also learnt from the crown code. It has realised that no umpire can focus his eyes on two different places at the one time so, as in crown, with distances of roughly 12 inches, umpires and markers are called in to assist in carrying out the measure.

One of the most respected referees in the crown green game is Terry Nichols from Cheshire. A fully qualified county referee since 1975 and Vice-Chairman and Cheshire representative on the British Crown Green Referees Society, he offers some words of advice for anyone wanting to qualify as a referee:

Competency is gained from experience and confidence and will not arrive overnight. Players will respect a referee if they are convinced he is unbiased at all times. Players should receive a fair deal at a measure and be allowed to express themselves on the green in their own style, within the laws of the game, and without any unnecessary interference from the said official.

The first golden rule is to remember who you are and why you are there on the green. Spectators have paid good money to watch bowling, not your refereeing. Become involved only when you are requested to do so by the players but, at the same time, always be aware, from a suitable distance, of what is going on in the game.

In more detail, here are a few tips:

1 **Answering the call 'Who's on?'** Whilst it is true that the primary function of a referee is not to tell bowlers 'who's on', and that you do not need 20–20 vision as a qualification to be a referee, you do need to be a reasonably good judge of a winning bowl. To put it another way, if you are a poor judge, you will lose credibility and will have some embarrassing moments. If you don't know, don't guess. Guesses are the prerogatives of spectators and book-makers. Never volunteer to tell bowlers who's on because you wish to become a John Motson – wait until you are asked. A referee must respect the fact that, in certain situations, a player does not ask because he knows who is on and he does not wish his opponent to know at that stage. The opponent has every right to ask if he or she wishes.

2 **Alertness and prevention**. Try to read games and to be in the right place at the right time. Don't stand in one corner when there are three jacks in the opposite corner. If there is more than one block on the green, try to be at an end when two bowls have been delivered – that is the most likely time that you will be asked who's on. If you prevent trouble, you don't have to sort it

out. Never talk to spectators. You will be forgiven for missing something if you are supervising a tight measure, but crucified if it is because you were talking.

3 **Measuring**. There is a simple philosophy on this subject. It is up to the two bowlers to decide who is on in the first place. If they cannot, and want to ask someone else to determine the outcome, then they must abide by the decision and might as well go for a cup of tea (without leaving the green, of course). This assumes that there are qualified officials in attendance. If the referee is satisfied that one bowl is in, everyone must abide by the decision. Never accede to a second measure unless you, the referee, requires it. The attitude of flat green bowlers walking away is something we must learn and, in the actual mechanics of the measuring, I like the flat green system of going back to the original bowl measured to double check that measures have not slipped.

4 **Wedges.** An interesting subject – there is a general reluctance to introduce them into the crown green game as there are too many existing Laws about not touching bowls. However, I do see a case for using them in instances where Law 35 applies.

5 **Sportsmanship.** Sportsmanship should prevail at all times. If a player is entitled to have his bowl back and does not wish to have it back, don't make him or her take it. We need all the sportsmanship we can get in the 1990s.

6 **Code of ethics.** We are now a Society – as a referee never talk in derogatory terms about another referee.

7 **Dress.** We have come a long way since the BCGRS was formed in 1985 and we now lay down guidelines of dress within our constitution for major competitions. We all know that the correct attire does not make a person a better referee, but we must move forward and continue to improve our image. How can we justifiably insist on players improving their dress, if referees do not meet the necessary standards?

8 **Lady referees**. It must take an awful lot of courage and self-confidence for a lady to referee a men's competition. If she is good enough, then she should be allowed to do so.

An amusing incident from the crown game relates to our problem of measuring with the feet. It is the habit of players to measure with their feet before calling up the referee. It was rumoured, and no-one will admit to who it was, that a player played with one shoe bigger than the other, so that when he measured his opponent's bowl he would use his smaller shoe, but when he measured his own he would use the larger one thus reducing the number of paces for his own bowl.

Another story relates to a referee who was officiating on one of his partner's matches. He apparently took elastic out to measure rather than string, making sure that his pal won the measures.

In crown green bowling, measuring is still a bone of contention. Different referees measure in different ways, leading to question marks about the accuracy of the measure. A new method has been suggested and this would state that when a bowl is less than ten inches from the jack, telescopic steel rods could be used. This method would ensure a far more accurate measure than simply using string.

With reference to the use of pegs in the crown green game, the husband and wife team who referee the Waterloo Handicap – Terry and Mary Ashcroft from Warrington – are totally against them, unlike Frank Kitchen and Terry Nichols. They feel that a 'leaning wood' is part of the gamble of measuring in the crown green game and that to put a support against the bowl is unethical.

THE FUTURE OF BOWLS

Keith Phillips

Bowls is one of those sports that can be sold world-wide at any time of the year. But in order to do this, there must be changes made to make it more attractive to the viewer. Certain rules and regulations must be reviewed and the bowlers must modernise their dress in order to make the game more appealing to television viewers.

There is no doubt that the sets game is far more exciting for both the viewers and the spectators, and that most top players now find it more exhilarating to play the sets game. This does not cast aspersions on the 21-up outdoor game played throughout the world, but it must be said that it is not suitable for television. In the Commonwealth Games and World championships, there is a week during which players compete in three to four hour matches before any semblance of a result is known. This must be good for the players, who sometimes play on 24 rinks at the same time, but it is felt that it is not good for selling the sport.

In travelling the world, the WIBC representatives have found a wonderful response to the sets game, with its determined length of matches making for exciting climaxes in the final. Because of this, there are plans for a brand-new club knockout competition to be played around the country and in sets in the near future. Each club will be represented by five or six players in singles matches against every other club. The belief is that this competition could make bowls a spectator sport every week.

There is no doubt that the young men coming into the game today want to play head to head singles or competitive bowls. Even players of the calibre of Allcock and Corsie, who have been brought up in the traditional game of bowls, get more satisfaction out of the sets game.

The WIBC are also considering using the sport to travel round the country, to gain more income from corporate hospitality. Ideas to use exhibitions to promote the game are also being developed. These areas could be extremely successful, but may need a bit of selling to begin with. A sponsoring company for a corporate hospitality day could take 64 customers to a bowls club. They could all play together with eight top-level players, have dinner with after-dinner speeches – bowls is famous for its raconteurs – and finish off with an international exhibition. The new bowls clubs, as well as many existing ones, already have six to eight rinks, restaurants and bar and entertainment facilities, which add up to ideal corporate hospitality venues. So, just as clay pigeon shooting, golf tournaments, snooker tournaments and go-carting competitions are now popular for corporate hospitality days, there is no reason whatsoever why bowls shouldn't be, with some of the top players, who would also be able to command some extra income, taking part.

This development may encourage more players to turn professional, which would automatically increase their standard of play and, therefore, be advantageous to everyone involved in the sport. With more professional players, clubs could have sponsored hospitality days for their own clubs and their own local sponsors.

Initially, the game needs to dress itself up more at club level. People have to accept that when they come to play, they don't just turn up from work, take their jackets and ties off, change their shoes and walk on to the rink. It's only recently that bowling clubs are providing changing rooms rather than just a locker to put shoes and jackets in. Nowadays, with the exposure of top players on television, people want to change into attractive sports gear and to look smart.

Although bowls is, at present, going through a 'hiccup' period on television the game is expanding at a very fast pace wherever there are rinks to play on. The UK, Australia and New Zealand are the back bone of the world-wide game. This year the number of countries who are members of the International Bowling Board has risen to 33. A number of these are European countries with potentially lucrative markets.

Regarding televising bowls, perhaps the sport was too lucky too early, getting three major television championships on BBC television and Granada television within the first two years of it being played indoors. The pessimists are beginning to make comments like 'things are looking bad, we've lost two tournaments.' However, there are now more competitions being broadcast by regional television companies than ever before, because they like the presentation of the sport, as well as the fact that it is not too expensive to cover. All the polls say that the public want even more coverage, and the WIBC firmly believe that bowls will become one of the major televised sports – whether it is on the BBC, ITV, Sky, BSB, Eurosport or Screensport. Also bowls is getting more hours of television now than it ever has previously, in Australia and New Zealand. The World Outdoor Championships in New Zealand in 1988 ran for 74 hours on the television networks.

One of the new areas that the WIBC is looking at is self-production, where they will be able to televise any one of their events to sell to any country in the world, starting initially in Europe and then the Far East.

The potential throughout the world is becoming an exciting prospect to all of us who love bowls and we wish every success to the WIBC in their future negotiations.

THE 1990 COMMONWEALTH GAMES

Keith Phillips

Men's Singles

At the start of the 14th Commonwealth Games, the question on everyone's lips was, could the 'maestro' of outdoor bowls, David Bryant, collect a record fifth gold medal? His opposition, which included Richard Corsie, David Corkill and that aggressive Australian, Rob Parella, looked formidable. David started out well, beating the 1986 Edinburgh bronze medallist, Garin Beare of Zimbabwe, 25–12 in the second round, after an easy win against Michael Smith of Guernsey, 25–9. He followed this in the third and fourth rounds with wins against Indonesia and Papua New Guinea. In round five, he came up against unbeaten Burney Gill of Canada, and had a comfortable win 25–15.

So far, so good, the 'script' was coming together. But in round six he faced one of his toughest matches yet against Ireland's David Corkill. Corkill's morning match had been against the new favourite, Rob Parella of Australia, and, after being 14–1 down, David had made a remarkable comeback to win 25–20. The two Davids faced each other, but Corkill couldn't maintain his morning form and Bryant came out on top, 25–14. All he now had to do was to beat Rob Parella to get to the gold.

The format for the gold, silver and bronze medals was a group of round robins, with the winner of each group playing each other for gold and

Rob Parella

silver, with the runners-up in each group playing for one bronze medal.

David Bryant was in group 'A' and unbeaten up to his final round robin match against Rob Parella. In group 'B' a new young star was coming through – 20-year-old Mark McMahon from Hong Kong – who was leading his group unbeaten. He had disposed of Richard Corsie of Scotland, Welshman John Price and one of the favourites from the start, the local hero Ian Dickinson. The scene was being set for a shoot-out between the master and the pupil – 58-year-old Bryant and 20-year-old McMahon.

As Bryant was unbeaten with nine shots in hand from the countdown of shots, he didn't have to beat Parella to get to the final. As long as he scored 16 shots he could afford to lose, as each game was 25 shots up, ie he could lose 25–16 and still get to the gold medal play-off.

Parella started out brilliantly and David Bryant couldn't seem to find the right line or weight. The Australian became more confident and, with some excellent drawing shots, moved into an almost unbeatable lead of 24–7. The Aussie was now cock-a-hoop, and performing his well-known antics after every shot he made. This must have got Bryant's determination up, because he suddenly found his line and weight and began clawing back. Bryant played some magnificent drawing shots to get back to 24–14. Then, within two shots of getting in the gold medal final, he laid a short jack (he had played long in his comeback) and Parella crept in to take the final 25–14.

The following morning, after many days of beautiful hot sunny weather there was an overcast sky. David Bryant, trying to hide his disappointment of not reaching the final, played Richard Corsie in the bronze medal play-off, a match of great potential between the World Outdoor Champion and the World Indoor Champion. Corsie took command of the game from the start, with some beautifully weighted draw shots, and was 10–3 ahead after eight ends.

Bryant then started a comeback and took three shots in the fifteenth end to pull back to 8–15. This didn't affect the World Indoor Champion's rhythm and he cruised to a commanding 20–10 lead after 20 ends. David wasn't bowling badly, in fact it was a vast improvement on his performance against Rob Parella, but the Scottish postman was bowling world class bowls. By this time the rain, which had begun as a light drizzle, was now getting heavier and water was lying on the edges of the green.

Despite this, after the next end, Bryant pulled one back, then another, and another and, in the 23rd end, scored a brilliant three shots to come within five shots of Richard Corsie. Were we going to see another spirited comeback from the 'maestro' who never seems to lie down? After 26 ends, David Bryant was within three shots, at 21–17, and Corsie knew he had a tough game on his hands. Drastic situations need drastic measures. Corsie pulled one out of the bag in the 27th end with a fantastic three shots to go into an unbeatable lead of 24–17, and took the bronze medal in the 28th end.

David Bryant, who had started out with a real chance of a record five gold medals in the Commonwealth Games, went home empty-handed and one wonders whether he will survive to take part in the next Games in 1994 at Victoria, Vancouver Island in Canada. He will definitely defend his World Outdoor title in 1992 at Worthing where his performance could decide his future.

During the lunch break, the rain came down in torrents and slowly began to flood the greens. The finalists came out at 2 pm to commence play but, after 15 minutes of deliberation, with the rain still coming down in buckets, the start was delayed. At 3.30 pm the greens were almost completely covered with water and the final was abandoned until the following morning. With the help of the morning sun and the very efficient groundstaff at Pakuranga the greens dried out ready for the gold medal play-off to begin.

The 'Hong Kong Kid', as Mark McMahon was affectionately christened by the media, at last faced the brilliant, flamboyant Aussie Parella in a final for gold and silver that caught the imagination of the bowling fraternity.

Parella went off to a flying start and quickly took a 7–0 lead but, unlike David Bryant, McMahon didn't let him race away. In the fifth end of this 25 shot final, the 'Hong Kong Kid' played some magnificent drawing shots and made three shots to pull back to 7–4 and start a wonderful spell of bowling.

In the eleventh, Parella took a two shot lead at 10–8 but then McMahon came back with some brilliant bowls to take the lead for the first time with three shots in the twelfth to make the score 11–10. After 16 ends, McMahon was still ahead at 14–2 and everyone at Pakuranga was still waiting to see the famous Parella firing shot – up to this point he had been trying to outdraw Mark. In the 17th end Parella took out McMahon's shot bowls to reduce the lead to 14–13 and then two more to take the lead again in the 18th, 15–14. Mark began to lose his near-perfect weight shots, first bowling too long, then too short. He didn't score another shot, letting Parella take his first Commonwealth Gold Medal with a comfortable score of 25–14. A sad ending for the 'Hong Kong Kid', but what an exciting prospect for the bowling world!

Afterwards, Rob Parella explained why he didn't resort to firing in the first part of the game. Overnight rain had made the green wet and, as Parella puts 110% effort into his driving shots, he was worried about slipping on the surface. In that case, Parella was fortunate that the sun had dried the green during the first half of the final because he was certainly being outdrawn until he started firing the 'Hong Kong Kid' out of the match.

Men's Pairs

With strong English and Welsh teams, Great Britain had two prospects for the gold medal in the pairs. England were in section A, with formidable opposition from Scotland, New Zealand and Australia, whilst Wales, on paper, had a much easier draw with only Canada looking dangerous.

England started off well, with Andy Thomson and Gary Smith having wins against Jersey, 28–25, Papua New Guinea, 33–13 and Northern Ireland, 24–14. The pairs matches were the best score after 21 ends and, in Round 5, England came up against their rivals Scotland. After a good start for England, the match developed into a fairly even game and after 14 ends England was leading 10–8. Then disaster struck for Gary and Andy as, in the 15th end, Angus Blair and Graham Robertson turned them over to take five shots and go in to a 13–10 lead. The English pair seemed to lose heart, and the Scots ended with a comfortable win of 19–13.

In Rounds 6 and 7, England had to win with as many shots as possible. Their other main rivals, Australia, were still unbeaten and New Zealand had only dropped one game, against Australia. England achieved this with wins against Zimbabwe, 34–13 and Guernsey, 25–20. In Round 8 they met the New Zealand pair of Rowan Brassey and Maurice Symes. A close match followed and, after 16 ends England were ahead 14–13. Then the sparks began to fly. In the 17th end New Zealand scored three to lead 16–14, then 17–14 and in the 19th end Gary and Andy hit back to draw level at 17–17. With two ends to go, there was nothing in it. Could England do it? Unfortunately the answer was 'no' and they lost by three shots, 20–17.

Luckily for England, Scotland caused an upset on the same green by beating the Australians for the gold in a very exciting match, 26–20. So England were still in with a chance of the bronze. They had to beat Australia in the final round but, due to bad weather the previous day, they had to play their third match of the day that evening.

This was the important tie against the Aussie pair of Ian Schuback and Trevor Morris and it finished in near darkness, with the English pair losing 24–16.

Surprisingly, Guernsey beat Scotland in the closest of finishes, 25–24, after Scotland had led 24–22 at the final end. New Zealand beat Northern Ireland 22–18. This meant that England were out of the medals and Australia were going for gold.

In Section B, Wales and Canada sailed comfortably through the early rounds unbeaten. In the sixth they came across one another for the 'crunch' match. Whoever won this one would surely go for the gold. Wales started well and led 4–3 after four ends, then Canada took over and, at the eleventh end, it was 10–10. In a magnificent end, Wales took six shots to lead 16–10 at the twelfth. After that, they slumped and only scored three shots in the next nine ends and Canada won 26–19.

This meant that Canada played for gold against Australia. In a one-sided final, Australia won comfortably 23–15. The bronze play-off between Wales and New Zealand was a much better match, with Robert Weale showing the packed stands a wonderful exhibition of pairs leading. Unfortunately his skip, William Thomas, wasn't up to standard on the day, which made the

119

match a close one. Wales were leading 17–16 after 17 ends and if ever Robert wanted his skip to perform, it was now. But it was not to be, and Maurice Symes out-bowled him, giving New Zealand the bronze, 24–17.

At the Press conference after the finals, the Australian pair paid the highest compliments to the English pair, saying that their most difficult match had been against Gary Smith and Andy Thomson in that late evening match. Their section was by far the toughest in the Games.

Men's Fours

England were again in a strong section in the fours, drawn with Australia, Hong Kong and the World Champions, Northern Ireland. In Section B, New Zealand and Scotland were favourites for the medals in an easier draw. Again it was the best of 21 ends.

England didn't get off to a good start. They defeated Zimbabwe in the first round 29–15, but came up against Australia in the second. Although leading 12–9 after 18 ends and looking good, they let the Aussies in for two counts of three shots to go behind 15–12. After 19 ends the Australians led 17–12 and, despite a spirited effort by the English team in the last two ends, they won 17–15. After four rounds, Northern Ireland were unbeaten, but then surprisingly dropped a match to Wales in the fifth in an extremely close game, 17–16.

In Round 6, the Australians must have wondered what had hit them as they went down to Swaziland 19–17 – it was the shock result of the Games at Pakuranga. This left the section wide open, and if England could win their next two matches, they would go for gold.

England met the World Champions, Northern Ireland, in Round 8. After 14 ends the Irish led easily at 16–6, but the English four began fighting back. From ends 15 to 20 Tony Allcock's team of John Ottaway, Gary Harrington and Roy Cutts took 12 shots to one from Jim Baker's team, and led 18–17 with one end to play. Could they do it? Once again the answer for England was 'no' but they managed a draw.

The situation looked bleak for England, because they had to beat Hong Kong convincingly to have the remotest chance of going for the bronze medal.

The Northern Ireland silver medallists, with the Scottish team, who took the gold in the Men's Fours

In the final round, Northern Ireland won comfortably against Australia, 17–14, so they were set for gold. England against Hong Kong was a tight match throughout, and at the 20th end Hong Kong were just in the lead at 16–14. In the final end, after the lead, second and third had bowled, England were five ahead. And who would have predicted what happened next? The Hong Kong skip was on his last bowl and, not renowned for his drawing ability, drew with weight, threading his way through the 14 bowls to take out England's bowls and turn over five shots to Hong Kong. Tony Allcock must have been shell-shocked as he fired with his last bowl and missed, and the match went to Hong Kong 21–14. So no medals at all for the England men's bowling team – a great disappointment, but they were very unlucky to come home empty-handed.

In Section B, Scotland came through unbeaten, so the gold medal shoot-out was between the Scots and Northern Ireland. Willie Wood, George Adrain, Ian Bruce and Denis Love faced up to Jim Baker's team of Sammy Allen, John McCloughlin and Rod McCutcheon.

The final was an unimpressive match, but good bowling from

skip Willie Wood and Ian Bruce set the Scottish team up to lead most of the match and they won the gold with a 19–14 win.

The bronze medal play-off was between Australia and New Zealand and an off-colour Australian fours team couldn't contain the exuberant New Zealand team led by Phil Skoglund, who had a great match at the back as skip. His opposing skip, Rex Johnston, was off form and couldn't put a foot right. So New Zealand won the bronze with an easy 21–13 win.

The Women's singles

England's Wendy Line, the gold medallist in Edinburgh in 1986, was expected to have a difficult passage in trying to defend her title. No-one in the bowling world, either men or women, nor the media, could have predicted the outcome of this event. Margaret Johnston of Northern Ireland was the favourite – after all she is the current World Indoor Singles Champion – and New Zealand's own Millie Khan looked a strong contender. But everybody overlooked a portly, genial competitor from Papua New Guinea by the name of Geua Tau.

Wendy Line was in Section A and her main rivals, on paper, were New Zealand and Australia. She played Audrey Hefford of Australia in her first match and had a lead of 17–4 after 14 ends. Then she began to falter and, after 24 ends, Hefford had levelled the match to 19–19. Wendy came back and took the match 25–19, but it wasn't an altogether totally convincing win by Wendy and this was proved when she lost by 25–24 against Vaiee Siaosi of Western Samoa in Round 2.

In Round 3, she lost again to Zimbabwe's Anne Morris 25–24, after being 20–13 down at end 18. She managed to pick herself up in Round 4 to beat Mark McMahon's mother, Rosemary, from Hong Kong with a comfortable score of 25–16, but struggled again in Round 5 against Flora Anderson of Botswana, just scraping home 25–24. In Round 7 she had an easy win over Emmeline Browning of Norfolk Island, 25–7, and then had to beat Millie Khan of New Zealand, to keep in with a chance of the bronze, in Round 8.

Millie looked certain for the gold play-off, as she was

Millie Khan with the gold medalist, Geua Tau

unbeaten, but Wendy gave her a fright. After being 19–14 down at the 21st end, she staged a Bryant-style comeback and levelled at 22–22 after 27 ends. But Millie Khan's precision drawing shots took her to a win at the 29th end, 25–22. Wendy Line, the defending champion, therefore, was out of the medal hunt and the home favourite, Millie Khan, topped the league in Section A to go for gold, with an unbeaten run of eight matches.

In Section B, the contest for a gold play-off was between Northern Ireland and Papua New Guinea. Margaret Johnston of Northern Ireland put up a spirited and skilful performance, but was played out of the gold by Geua Tau who went through the section unbeaten and, needless to say, was the only one to beat Margaret, who had to be satisfied with getting to the bronze medal play-off.

Janet Ackland of Wales, the World Outdoor Champion, had a disappointing Games. Had she beaten Geua Tau in the last round of the robin, she would have let Margaret Johnston in for the gold medal play-off. But nobody, it seemed, could do anything against this popular lady from Papua New Guinea and Janet was trounced 25–6. So, the gold medal play-off was between Geua Tau and Millie Khan, and our own Margaret Johnston was going for bronze against Audrey Hefford from Australia. Margaret was in great form in this important match and had an easy win by 25–15 to take the bronze medal.

The final for gold and silver medals was eagerly awaited by the home crowd, who had started packing the stands on green D at Pakuranga during the morning matches for the bronze medals. By the start of the match there wasn't a seat left.

When Millie Khan stepped on to the green, there was a tremendous roar from the enthusiastic audience, and a home win seemed to be on the cards. Remember, both ladies had come through to the final unbeaten and Geua Tau was obviously no pushover. After four ends Geua was on top 3–2, and the next six ends belonged to Millie who gradually gained an 8–6 lead at the 10th end.

Geua was beginning now to get her favourite forehand drawing shot going and in the 15th end was bowling with absolute precision to go into a lead of 11–10. In the 18th she scored a three, and a four in the 19th to go into an unassailable lead of

20-11. Millie tried desperately to get back into the game and, with the crowd willing her on with tremendous enthusiasm, she pegged back two shots in the next end. But Geua's extremely cool temperament was not to be disturbed and she went on to win the gold with a score of 25-18. It was a great exhibition of forehand drawing by the Papua New Guinea champion and greatly appreciated by the home crowd.

Women's pairs

England and Northern Ireland were in Section A of the Women's Pairs competition, together with Wales, while Scotland were up against New Zealand in Section B.

The England pairing of Mary Price and Jayne Roylance were expected to win a medal and, true to form, only lost one match – to Winnona Butcher and Judith Penfold from Zimbabwe – drawing 22-22 with Kathy Panap and Kathy Sigimet of Papua New Guinea. Once again, a slip of concentration against an unfancied Zimbabwe pair cost the English couple a gold medal chance. This gave Australia the top place to go into the gold medal play-off.

In Section B, Scotland nearly made it to the gold play-off, as they finished level with New Zealand. Both only lost one match, but New Zealand had the highest shot average and, therefore, went on to play Australia in the gold play-off, whilst England and Scotland were left with playing for the bronze.

The England v Scotland match was basically a one-sided affair, apart from the eighth end when Frances Whyte and Sarah Gourlay scored a magnificent six shots to bring Scotland level at 8-8. Once again, England took command and went on to win the bronze 22-14.

The final was between Australia's Edda Bonutto and Maureen Hobbs, with New Zealand being represented by Judy Howatt and Marie Watson. The Aussies took hold of the game from the start, and went into a lead of 12-8 after 12 ends. Then the Kiwis, with noisy support from a patriotic crowd, began to take control. After 18 ends it was anyone's match, with New Zealand in the lead by only two shots, 15-13. In the 19th, Judy and Marie scored a pulverising four shots to go further into the lead by 19-13. This completely shattered the Aussie pair and

New Zealand took the gold 23–13. A happy victory for the home crowd.

Women's fours

In the final event of the Commonwealth Games Bowling competition, England, Scotland and Wales were together in Section A, with Northern Ireland not putting in a team.

England lost three matches and, therefore, didn't qualify for a medal, but Scotland, losing two, went for the bronze. The leading team in Section A was, once again, New Zealand who went for gold. In Section B, Australia qualified for the gold play-off and Hong Kong for the bronze.

So the bronze play-off was between Scotland and Hong Kong. The Scottish four were hoping to emulate the men's fours by winning a medal. In a fascinating match, Scotland were ahead all the time, except for two ends – the first and the last. The Hong Kong four took the first end 2–0, Scotland scored four shots in the second and led all the way to the final end. After 17 ends Scotland led 20–14 and then didn't score a shot for the rest of the match. At the 20th end Scotland led 20–19 and, in a dramatic final, Hong Kong managed to hold two shots and win the bronze 21–20. The Scots four were incredulous and the Hong Kong ladies did jubilant dances down the rink.

The final was another tussle between the Aussies and the Kiwis, with one of the closest matches of the Commonwealth Games. From the start to the finish there was never more than three or four shots between them, and in the 20th end they were level at 18–18. In the 21st and final end, the Australian four came through to win the gold with two shots at 20–18.

It was my privilege to be at the 14th Commonwealth Games as the BBC TV Producer at the Bowls and I witnessed some exciting, dramatic and first class games of bowls. Nothing but good can come out of this event for the game of bowls and it certainly helped enormously to promote the game throughout the world. One sad note – the English men's team, fancied so much for two or three medals, came home empty-handed, but with a little bit of luck going their way they could have comfortably won them.

All in all, a wonderful two weeks of competition.

TOURNAMENT RESULTS UP TO 1990

WORLD INDOOR SINGLES CHAMPIONSHIP 1979–1989

	Winners		Runners-up	
1979	David Bryant	21	Jim Donnelly	14
1980	David Bryant	21	Philip Chok	15
1981	David Bryant	21	John Thomas	18
1982	John Watson	21	Jim Baker	13
1983	Bob Sutherland	21	Burnie Gill	10
1984	Jim Baker	21	Nigel Smith	18
1985	Terry Sullivan	21	Cecil Bransky	18
1986	Tony Allcock	21	Phil Skoglund	15
1987	Tony Allcock	5	David Bryant	4
1988	Hugh Duff	5	Wynne Richards	0
1989	Richard Corsie	5	Willie Wood	0

CIS UK INDOOR SINGLES CHAMPIONSHIP 1983–1989

	Winners		Runners-up	
1983	David Bryant	3	Bob Sutherland	0
1984	Terry Sullivan	5	Tony Allcock	4
1985	Jim Baker	5	John Watson	2
1986	Stephen Rees	5	David Bryant	4
1987	Tony Allcock	5	David Corkill	4
1988	Gary Smith	5	Richard Corsie	3
1989	David Bryant	3	David Corkill	2

JACK HIGH 1978–1986

	Winners		Runners-up	
1978	David Bryant	21	Dick Folkins	12
1979	David Bryant	21	David McGill	11
1980	Bill Moseley	21	David McGill	16
1981	Bill Moseley	21	David McGill	14
1982	David Bryant	21	John Snell	12
1983	George Souza	21	David Bryant	19
1984	David Bryant	21	Peter Bellis	16
1985	David Bryant	21	Cecil Bransky	12
1986	David Bryant	21	Ian Dickison	19

The Waterloo 1907–1989

	Winners	*Runners-up*
1907	Jas Rothwell West Leigh	T. Richardson South Shore
1908	Geo. Beatty Burnley	James Southern Darwen
1909	Tom Meadows West Leigh	W.H. Andrews Stalybridge
1910	No Handicap	
1911	John Peace Huddersfield	F. Walmsley Blackburn
1912	T. Lowe Westhoughton	C. Farrington Howe Bridge
1913	Gerard Hart Blackrod	R. Hart Blackrod
1914	John Rothwell Atherton	F. Percival Wilmslow
1915	W. Fairhurst Standish	Walter Simms Aspull
1916	J. Parkinson Oldham	E. Hall Platt Bridge
1917	G. Barnes Westhoughton	H. Hemingway Burnley
1918	W. Simms Aspull	J. Pimblett Pemberton
1919	Len Moss Denton	T. Richardson South Shore
1920	E. Whiteside Lytham	D. Brown Lostock Hall
1921	J. Bagot South Shore	Walter Guest Bury
1922	W.A. Smith Old Trafford	Geo. Barnes Westhoughton
1923	J. Martin Westhoughton	Geo. Barnes Westhoughton
1924	Rowland Hill Brynn	R. Banks Bolton
1925	Jack Cox Blackpool	T. Whittle Ashton-in-Makerfield
1926	T. Roscoe Blackpool	T. Cornwell Chorley
1927	H. Waddecar Midge Hall	Seth Mason Blackrod
1928	T. Whittle Ashton-in-Makerfield	J. Meadows South Shore

	Winners	*Runners-up*
1929	Chas. Halpin Blackpool	J. Hart Hollinwood
1930	J. Chadwick Westhoughton	W. Park Preston
1931	A. Gleave Warrington	W. Grace Blackpool
1932	T.E. Booth West Didsbury	T. Davies Atherton
1933	A. Ogden Failsworth	R. Thomas Hindley
1934	W. Derbyshire Burnley	W. Hargreaves Blackburn
1935	C. Roberts Fearnhead	R. Thomas Hindley
1936	H. Yates Preston	F. Wolstencroft North Shore
1937	A. King Windermere	T. Suttie Blackburn
1938	J.W. Whitter Standish	D. Jacks Keersley
1939	Abandoned	
1940	H. Holden Blackpool	J. Swithenbank Blackpool
1941	W.J. Wilcock St Helens	W. Finch Blackpool
1942	T. Bimson Hardhorn	J. Ormond Blackpool
1943	S. Ivell Little Hulton	J. Stevenson Blackpool
1944	T. Tinker Huddersfield	T. Richardson Blackpool
1945	W. Grace Blackpool	D. Ayrton Blackpool
1946	C. Parkinson Pemberton	T. Bimson Hardhorn
1947	W. Dalton Fleetwood	R. Robinson Preston
1948	A.E. Ringrose Bradford	W. Derbyshire Newtown
1949	J. Egan Birkdale	J. Lawton Lancaster
1950	H. Finch Blackpool	W. Green Blackrod
1951	J. Waterhouse Middleton	T. Bimson Hardhorn

	Winners	Runners-up
1952	L. Thompson St Helens	W. Worthington Droylsden
1953	B. Kelly Hyde	H. Taberner Altrincham
1954	B. Kelly Hyde	A. Holden Fulwood
1955	J. Heyes Aspull	G. Bromley Blackpool
1956	J. Sumner Blackpool	H. Pennington Whiston
1957	W. Lacy Wigan	T. Bimson St Anne's
1958	F. Salisbury Preston	W. Carter Rainhill
1959	W. Dawber Wrightington	H. Wallwork Pendlebury
1960	H. Bury Blackpool	J. Featherstone Leigh
1961	J. Featherstone Leigh	C. Taylor Blackpool
1962	J. Collier Pendleton	Tom Mayor Bolton
1963	T. Mayor Bolton	D. Hogarth Lytham
1964	W.B. Heinkey Birmingham	L. Taylor Swinton
1965	J. Pepper Salford	A. Wood Broughton
1966	R. Collier Little Hulton	F. Mountford Rochdale
1967	Eric Ashton Towyn	D. Kirkham Chorlton-cum-Hardy
1968	Billy Bennett Warrington	A. Thompson Carleton
1969	G.T. Underwood Blackpool	C.E. Jackson Andsell
1970	Jack Everitt Willenhall	A. Howarth Royton
1971	J. Bradbury Romiley	S.V. Ellis Blackpool
1972	N. Burrows Withington	W. Brindle Bolton
1973	A. Murray Partington	J. Hadfield Preston

	Winners		*Runners-up*	
1974	W. Houghton Freckleton		S.V. Ellis Blackpool	
1975	J. Colien Bury		S.A. Rogers Davyhulme	
1976	K. Illingworth Blackpool		S. Buckley Chadderton	
1977	L. Barrett Whitefield		L. Gilfedder Warrington	
1978	A. Murray Partington		W.H. Smith Wirral	
1979	B. Duncan Leigh		A. Broadhurst Aspull	
1980	V. Lee Blackpool		G. Vernon Winsford	
1981	R. Nicholson Brighouse		B. Prolze Altrincham	
1982	D. Mercer Stockport		K. Strutt Oldham	
1983	S. Frith Weaverham		B. Henstead Wigan	
1984	S. Ellis Kirkham		J. Lees Walton-le-Dale	
1985	T. Johnstone Manchester		A. Thompson Mirfield	
1986	B. Duncan Leigh		J. Sykes Mirfield	
1987	B. Duncan Leigh	21	R. Eaton Holmes Chapel	11
1988	I. Gregory Bolton	21	G. Cookson Winsford	13
1989	B. Duncan Leigh	21	K. Wainwright Warrington	12

TOP CROWN 1968–1988

BBC Crown Green Masters

	Winners		*Runners-up*	
1968	W. Dawber	21	Dick Meyrick	12
1969	Roy Armson	21	Larry Greene	5
1970	No Competition			
1971	No Competition			
1972	Dennis Mercer	15	Jack Everitt	9

TOP CROWN

	Winners		*Runners-up*	
1973	Brian Duncan	21	Dennis Mercer	6
1974	Brian Duncan	21	Fred Hulme	15
1975	Dennis Mercer	21	Brian Duncan	16
1976	Tony Poole	21	Norman Dawkes	12
1977	Roy Price	21	Dennis Mercer	16
1978	Gene Bardon	21	Roy Nicholson	19
1979	Brian Duncan	21	Noel Burrows	10

TOP CROWN – PAIRS TOURNAMENT

	Winners		*Runners-up*	
1980	Noel Burrows and Mike Leach	21	Terry Turner and Keith Widdowson	16
1981	Gene Bardon and Roy Nicholson	21	Brian Duncan and Norman Fletcher	13
1982	Allan Thompson and Robert Hitchen	15	Brian Duncan and Norman Fletcher	14
1983	Ken Strutt and David Blackburn	15	Robert Hitchen and Allan Thompson	11
1984	Eddie Hulbert and Tommy Johnstone	21	Ken Strutt and David Blackburn	15
1985	Robert Hitchen and Roy Nicholson	21	Frank Kitchen and Michael Eccles	17
1986	Brian Duncan and Norman Fletcher	21	Tommy Johnstone and Eddie Hulbert	19
1987	Roy Armson and Noel Burrows	21	Gerald Gregson and Alan Shacklady	10
1988	Ken Strutt and Tommy Heyes	21	Peter Varney and Bob Gilfillan	20

THE COMMONWEALTH GAMES 1990

Gold	*Silver*	*Bronze*

MEN'S SINGLES – 25 SHOTS UP

Rob Parella	Mark McMahon	Richard Corsie
Australia	Hong Kong	Scotland

MEN'S PAIRS – BEST OF 21 ENDS

Ian Schuback	George Boxwell	Maurice Symes
Trevor Morris	Alf Wallace	Rowan Brassey
Australia	Canada	New Zealand

MEN'S FOURS – BEST OF 21 ENDS

Willie Wood	Jim Baker	Phil Skoglund
George Adrain	Sam Allen	Peter Shaw
Ian Bruce	Rod McCutcheon	Stewart McConnell
Denis Love	John McCloughlin	Kevin Darling
Scotland	Northern Ireland	New Zealand

WOMEN'S SINGLES – 25 SHOTS UP

Geua Tau	Millie Khan	Margaret Johnston
Papua New Guinea	New Zealand	Northern Ireland

WOMEN'S PAIRS – BEST OF 21 ENDS

Judy Howatt	Edda Bonutto	Mary Price
Marie Watson	Maureen Hobbs	Jayne Roylance
New Zealand	Australia	England

WOMEN'S FOURS – BEST OF 21 ENDS

Dorothy Roche	Marlene Castle	Eva Ho
Audrey Rutherford	Adrienne Lambert	Angela Chau
Daphne Shaw	Lynette McLean	Natty Rozario
Marion Stevens	Rhoda Ryan	Jenny Wallis
Australia	New Zealand	Hong Kong

GLOSSARY

Backhand: When for the right-handed player the bowl is delivered so that the curve of the bowl is from left to right towards its objective.

Bias: That which is inbuilt into the bowl, which causes the bowl to travel in a curve.

Block or Stopper: A wood delivered with enough pace to stop short of the objective, in the hope that it will prevent an opponent being able to play a certain shot.

Dead End: An end which is considered not to have been played and for which no score is recorded. It can happen as a result of the jack being driven out of the confines of the playing area.

Dead Wood or Bowl: A bowl which comes to rest in the ditch, or is knocked into the ditch and is not a toucher. Or a bowl that comes to rest outside the confines of the rink, either in its course or by being knocked there.

Ditch: The green is surrounded by a depression whose edge marks the boundary of the playing surface. Measurements of the ditch need to conform to the laws of the game.

Fire or Drive: There are various reasons for such a shot, but it is a shot where the bowl is delivered at a very fast pace.

Foot Fault: The rear foot must be on or above the mat at the moment of delivery, or the player could incur a penalty.

Forehand: When for the right-handed player the bowl is delivered so that the curve of the bowl is from right to left towards its objective.

The Head: The jack and as many bowls as have been played at any stage of any end. Bowls in the head may be on the rink or in the ditch.

Jack or Kitty: The white ball towards which play is directed.

Live Bowl/Wood: Any bowl that comes to rest within the confines of the rink and allowing for conditions as laid down by the laws of the game. Or any toucher in the ditch.

Long Jack: The greatest distance allowed from the front edge of the mat to the jack.

The Marker: A person who in a game of singles undertakes to see the game played according to the rules, will mark all touchers, centre the jack and measure as well as keeping the score.

The Mat: A bowler must make his delivery from the mat (the size of the mat is 24in by 14in).

A Plant Shot: Where a player bowls his wood to strike other woods which could be in line, and thus gain his objective.

Push and Rest: The bowling of a bowl of sufficient pace or weight that it pushes a bowl from its position so that that position is taken by the last bowl delivered.

Rink: A rectangular area of the green not more than 19ft or less than 18ft wide on which play takes place.

Short Jack: The shortest distance allowed from the front edge of the mat to the jack.

The Shot: The bowl that finishes nearest to the jack at any stage of play.

Shoulder of the Green: That point on the green where the bowl begins to curve inwards towards its objective.

String: Normally a green 'string' drawn tightly along the green to define the boundaries of the rink.

Toucher: A bowl which during its course has touched the jack.

Toucher in the Ditch: A toucher as above which has fallen into the ditch shall be a 'live' wood, but not if it has come to rest outside the confines of the rink.

Trail the Jack: A bowl played in order to move the jack to another position on the rink.

CROWN GREEN

Blocker: Bowl bowled short of a length so as to impede line from footer to jack or short bowl.

Cobbing: Northern term used to describe a certain type of delivery used when the green is waterlogged. Bowl is thrown over puddles. Not elegant but effective.

Footer: Circular rubber/plastic disc from which delivery of jack and bowls must be made.

Length Bowl: Bowl has finished its traction and is level with the length of the jack.

No Weight: Term used to indicate that player is bowling consistently long or short of the jack.

Shunting: When opponent has bowled short, bowling up the same line/land as opponent's bowl to push his bowl nearer the jack.

Stamping: Illegal use of feet stamping near to running bowl to accelerate or promote greater distance.